FREEDOM UNDER PLANNING

Freedom
UNDER
PLANNING

BARBARA WOOTTON

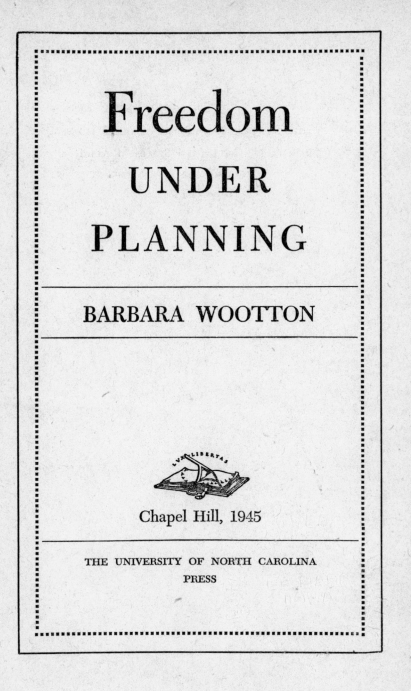

Chapel Hill, 1945

THE UNIVERSITY OF NORTH CAROLINA
PRESS

Copyright, 1945, by

Preface

THIS essay is an attempt to say a little on a very large, very pressing and generally neglected subject. I hope it may be read at least as much as an appeal to others to join in tackling that subject, as for any positive contribution that these pages may themselves contain.

That contribution would have been even less adequate than it is, or indeed might never have been made at all, had it not been for five people, to whom special thanks are due: to Bill and Gwen Hilliard for providing refuge from the household chores and bombs that are so detrimental to writing; to Leonora Simeon for making an impossible manuscript into a clean typescript; to Barbara Kyle for checking many irritating details and contributing many constructive criticisms; and to my husband, George Wright, for daily experience in the marriage of freedom and planning.

I have also to thank Professor F. A. Hayek for his kindness in letting me have an early view of his *Road to Serfdom*. Much of what I have written is devoted to criticism of the views put forward by Professor Hayek in this and other books. Intellectual controversy on serious practical and political issues is not always conducted in an atmosphere of personal goodwill. It is on that account the greater pleasure to express here my appreciation and reciprocation of the unchanging friendliness of Professor Hayek's attitude.

Finally it is a pleasure to acknowledge my perpetual

debt to the Librarian and staff of the Fulham Public Library, whose helpfulness, freedom from red tape, and relentless struggle against the book famine are a magnificent demonstration of the standards of elasticity and efficiency attainable in the public services. Without their continual support I should be a great deal more ignorant than I am.

B. W.

London, October, 1944.

Contents

FREEDOM UNDER PLANNING

CHAPTER I

Introduction *

I

THE FREEDOMS that matter in ordinary life are definite and concrete; and they change with the changing ways of different ages and different civilizations. Freedom today might mean, for instance, freedom to ask for your cards and sweep out of an objectionable job; freedom to say what you think of the government in language of your own choosing; freedom to join, or to refuse to join, the Transport and General Workers' Union; freedom to start a rival Union on your own; freedom to be a Freemason, a Catholic or a Plymouth Brother; freedom from concentration camps, official spying and detention without trial; freedom to stand for Parliament or the Parish Council on any program that you like; freedom to strike or not to strike; freedom to wear a nightdress or pyjamas as you prefer. No one would suggest that all these freedoms are of equal importance; nor do these examples necessarily cover all the freedoms that we actually have, can have, or ought to have. The relative value of different freedoms, and the conditions under which they can in fact be realized are difficult and debatable matters, and are, in

* The author, writing in England, has drawn her illustrative material from British life.

3

fact, debated in the pages that follow. But a random list of typical contemporary freedoms is useful as a reminder that free*dom* has to be perpetually reinterpreted into free*doms*. You can philosophize endlessly about freedom; but in daily life it is freedoms that you want. This book would in fact have been called *Freedoms Under Planning*, had not the title been so impossibly ugly.

At the same time all freedoms have a common quality—the quality, in fact, of freedom. If the discussion is to be practical and realistic, it is necessary to have a working notion of what this particular quality is. For the purpose of this book, which is severely practical, freedom may be simply defined as ability to do what you want. Behind every word in that definition there lurks, admittedly, a mass of philosophic doubts and subtleties. In practice one must turn a blind eye to these, and build on the assumption that in ordinary life most people recognize the difference between ability to do what they want, and inability to do this. Lack of freedom, at all events, is unmistakable enough. Most of us know only too well the peculiar emotion of frustration by which denial or deprivation of freedom is accompanied.

Taking this earthy, commonsense view of the nature of freedom, we admittedly bypass the complex issues raised by the child who, on returning to a progressive school after the holidays, is said to have asked: "Mummy, shall I still have to do what I want to do?" Equally we suspend judgment on the implications of the (no doubt apocryphal) Treasury Minute [1] which declared that: "It is one thing to compel an officer to retire voluntarily, another to permit him to retire compulsorily. Please keep the

1. Quoted by Mallalieu: *Pass to you, Please*, p. 105.

two distinct, lest worse confusion befall." What is more important, we deny the validity, for all practical purposes, of any distinction between what people want to do, and what they "really" want to do. Any such distinction is extremely dangerous, and may be the cloak for some of the most wicked, because the most insidious, attacks upon freedom. For sooner or later what I "really" want to do turns out to be a polite paraphrase for what you think I ought to want to do. But freedom means freedom to do what *I* want, and not what anybody else wants me to want—or else it has no meaning at all. How my wants come to be what they are is, no doubt, the result of a complex social and personal process which had best be left to the psychologist to explore. So far as freedom is concerned, what people want to do must be taken as something to be discovered, not changed.

There is another reason for emphasizing this. Freedom for everybody to do what he wants is not necessarily the sole purpose of organized society. There may be other admirable social ends which conflict with, or demand, limitations upon freedom. The possibility of one such conflict and the methods by which it may be resolved is indeed the theme of this book. It is, however, possible to use the word freedom in such a comprehensive way that it covers practically every conceivable social end. For instance, a full belly and an educated mind are commonly thought of today as good things in themselves; and the view is widely held that it is the business of the state to see that people are in fact in a position to enjoy these blessings. But the use of the terms "freedom from want" and "freedom from ignorance" to describe these desirable conditions is liable to confuse any serious discussion of freedom, and to obscure real problems. For in this way the term freedom is easily stretched so wide as to be emptied of distinctive meaning; and the very possibility of conflict, real enough in experience, between freedom and other praiseworthy social ends is disposed of by a verbal trick. The fact is, of course, that people's freedom—their ability to do what they want—is affected in many and complex ways by nearly every kind of organized social activity. Thus, one of the reasons for desiring a full stomach is that, if your stomach is empty, you will not be free to do anything else until you have filled it. But it is absurd to infer from this either that freedom consists in, and is identical with, a state of repletion, or that the limitation which the pangs of hunger impose on your freedom is the only reason for wishing to be rid of those pangs. A condition of well-fed, well-housed, well-clad, even well-entertained, slavery is not an imaginary impossibility. It is only too possible. But it is not freedom. Freedom should not be defined in terms which, even by implication, deny the possibility that a high degree of material well-being may be accompanied by deprivation of freedom. Prisoners would not become free men even if they were looked after as well as race horses.

Where all the terms are so highly charged with political bias it is necessary to be unusually careful about definitions. What then is meant by planning? Planning, in the sense that is relevant here, may be defined as the conscious and deliberate choice of economic priorities by some public authority. Economic activity consists essentially of choice. Shall I spend this shilling on a pint of mild or send a greetings telegram to my mother on her birthday? Shall I buy a house or rent one? Shall this field be plowed, left as pasture or built over? The first two of these choices may be said to be concerned with priorities of consumption, the third with priorities of production. There must of course always be some connection between the two kinds of choice, since it is not possible to consume that which is not produced. In the long run the pattern of consumption, apart from saving and waste (both of which, by a stretch of language not greater than is customary in the peculiar vocabulary of economics, may be included as special forms of consumption) is identical with the pattern of production. It does not, however, follow that whoever determines the general pattern of production also necessarily decides just exactly what each individual will consume.

It is this planning of production which is the heart of the matter. Since it is not possible to produce indefinite quantities of everything in a given place, as for instance in this island, there must be choice, and there must be priority. You cannot feed a cow off a suburban villa; to that extent there is on every acre a conflict between agriculture and building, in which one must eventually give way to the other. In every case, therefore, priorities of production must somehow be eventually determined. In the world as we know it there are, in principle, two ways, in one or other or both of which these questions can be settled. They can be settled consciously and deliberately as part of a plan, or they can be left to settle themselves through the higgling of the market (more politely known as the market mechanism). In the latter case, the final picture emerges as the unpremeditated result of the decisions of perhaps thousands of people, each of whom is concerned only with his own particular part (and that often a very tiny one) of the whole. Planning, on the other hand, implies that there is a known target to be aimed at. In the Soviet Union, the planned output of coal, for instance, in the third year of the second five-year plan, was 110 million tons. The output actually realized was 108.9 million tons.[2] The plan figure thus stands as a measure by which to judge the results that were in fact recorded. In this country, at about the same time, the annual output of coal was 226.5 million tons. Nobody planned that. It happened.

It will be noticed that I have confined the term planning to the determination of priorities by a public authority. In this context "public authority" means a state or government (with police and military power to give effect to its decisions if necessary); or some other body which the state has itself created, or to which it has expressly devolved certain rights and duties—such as the London County Council, created by Act of Parliament in 1888, or the London Passenger Transport Board, also created by Act of Parliament, in 1933. This limitation on the meaning of planning is a matter of convenience. In ordinary speech the decision to put a shilling on a horse may well be spoken of as part of an *individual's* economic plan; and in some instances large-scale economic planning may be undertaken by other than public bodies. The total output of certain chemicals in this country, for instance, must be fairly closely planned by Imperial Chemical Industries. The policy of that firm will make a most significant difference to the total. As has been said, however, the uncoordinated small-scale plans of individuals gen-

2. State Planning Commission of the U.S.S.R., *The Second Five-Year Plan*, p. xxiv.

erally add up to a result which is completely unplanned; and the large-scale planning of private monopolies raises issues which, though alarming and important enough, are different from those characteristic of what is coming to be called a "planned economic system."

The use of the phrase "economic system" must not be held to imply that the world is neatly divided into planned economies on the one hand, and unplanned economies on the other. Planning is a matter of degree. It is nowhere completely absent nor does it anywhere cover 100 per cent of all economic activity. Yet the span that divides the Soviet Union from New Deal America may be wide enough to justify the use, as a convenient shorthand, of the respective labels "planned" and "unplanned" *"system."* Even in the Soviet Union, the collective farmer can grow and sell what he likes as he likes on his own modest allotment, not bothering about anybody's plans but his own. In real life a pure economy is as improbable as a pure race. Economic hybrids are scarcely less varied than biological.

If, for practical purposes, economic planning is to mean *state* economic planning, it follows that, in the present stage of political development, plans must be confined within national boundaries. M. Stalin's government can make and execute most comprehensive plans of production throughout the vast areas over which they rule. If they wish to extend the geographical scope of their plans, they must first find some way of incorporating the territory of their neighbors into the Soviet Union. International economic planning is indeed possible in the sense that independent governments may agree to co-operate in certain economic activities, or create joint organs to regulate the output of particular commodities. The production of rubber and other raw materials was internationally planned in this way before the war. The status of plans of this kind is, however, necessarily quite different from that of those imposed by a government within the limits of its own authority. If the members of the Blankshire County Council fail to carry out their statutory duty to provide education for the children of the county in accordance with plans laid down by Parliament, they will personally be compelled by force of law to conform, or to get out: and it will be no use pleading that the people of Blankshire, holding as they do that ignorance is bliss, do not therefore wish to be bothered with education. But if the Dutch government took a dislike to the rubber control scheme and decided to disregard its provisions, they would have been amenable to no effective authority. The Dutch electors might refuse at their next opportunity to re-elect a government that had proved so careless of its bond. But that would still be a matter only between Dutch and Dutch. The remaining parties to the agreement, outside Holland, must confine themselves to protests, or in the last resort to economic or military sanctions directed, not against the offending members of the Netherlands government, but against the Dutch people as a whole. If the Blankshire County Council ignores the law, there is no question of blockading or bombing the County.

This difference between the activities of governments inside and outside their own boundaries is as plain as a pikestaff as well as quite fundamental. But it is sometimes forgotten in practice. The members of an international planning authority (the phrase, in a world of still sovereign states, is actually a contradiction in terms) are either severally responsible to the several governments by whom they have been appointed (each one of which may at any time change its mind about the whole business); or else they are responsible to no one—self-appointed dictators in fact. Incidentally, this dilemma necessarily tempers, though it does not invalidate, the hope that international political unity will eventually emerge from, rather than precede, international economic integration. For present purposes its chief significance is that it unavoidably limits the scope of the discussion. A plan which has the force of law is at most, as things are, a national plan. A planned economy can only mean an economy which is predominantly planned by the government of one state (or its appointees) for the people of that state. This of itself creates certain special problems affecting freedom, different from those which would be raised by the world-wide plans of a government of world-wide authority.

It is perhaps worth adding that state planning of priorities in production, even if it covered much the greater part of our economic life, is not necessarily identical with socialism. Socialism is generally held to mean (among other things) public ownership and operation of industry. Now, in theory at least, it is quite possible for the state to make all major decisions about how much of what is to be produced, without itself undertaking anything approaching the whole of that production. That is indeed, near enough, what happens in war. Production and priorities are officially planned and are carried out to government order; but by no means all these orders are executed in firms in which the workers are directly government employees. In principle, therefore, the distinction between socialism and economic planning is parallel with the distinction between doing something yourself and telling, or paying, somebody else to do it. How far such planning without socialism would be practicable except in the special circumstances of war is a question to which experience gives as yet no clear answer.[3] The convinced socialist (if he can be persuaded to proceed beyond dogmatic assertion that the two are inherently incompatible) will argue that government plans which are not also government-executed will either founder on the rocks of vested interest, or be wrecked by exploitation. In a world where business men are accustomed to make their own plans with an eye on their own or their firm's profit, very strong pressure may be put on the government to frame its own programs to suit the wishes at least of those private concerns which are large enough to make themselves heard. If this fails, the business world, it is said, will bring up a large armory of weapons with which to defeat the substance, while accepting the letter, of a government program; and finally the apparatus of controls (price regulation, profit limitation, quotas, perhaps concentration of industry, to name only a few complexities) which government will need to establish to prevent such tricks—will prove so formidable that in the end the conclusion that it would be more sensible to do the job yourself will become irresistible. That is, anyhow, how it looks to the socialist. What people will put up with in the war, he will say, is no guide to what can be done with them in peace; and, even in war, it cannot be said that the enforcement of the controls necessary for comprehensive planning is either frictionless or easy. The amount of effort which is devoted to circumventing government regulations seems

3. This point is discussed further in Chapter VIII.

to be considerable: the amount of effort devoted to circumventing such efforts to circumvent the law is even greater. And even so there are still black markets and prosecutions. If this is what happens in war, the socialist will write off the possibilities of public planning without public production in peacetime, when the danger and the glory are past, as hopeless. Necessarily, however, this remains a question of opinion. Nor is it certain that the answer is the same for all communities at all times. Business men vary both in their predatory qualities, and in their sense of public responsibility. Until the weight of experience is conclusive one way or the other, the problems of freedom under planning must be treated as distinct from those of freedom under socialism. But the prudent will remember the possibility that the one may lead to the other.

II

I have said that it is freedoms, rather than freedom, which matters. It may clear the ground a little further if these freedoms are roughly classified. We may distinguish civil, cultural, political and economic freedoms. The civil and cultural are much the most difficult to define with precision. Cultural liberty includes many varied freedoms of action and expression, while civil freedoms cover chiefly various legal, or judicial, rights which are particularly important to persons rightly or wrongly accused of offenses against the law. Among the former free speech and religious freedom are generally ranked high: among the latter we count in this country *habeas corpus,* and the right to trial by a tribunal which is not also a party to the prosecution. Political freedoms are those which have to do with the right to choose, to change, or to influence, the government in power. Freedom to vote or to form an opposition political party are two practical examples. Economic freedoms are those primarily concerned with getting and spending an income, or with the use and ownership of property. It is obvious that this classification is not watertight. Freedom of speech, for example, if one wishes to speak on political topics, overlaps the boundary between civil and political freedoms. Freedom to join a Trade Union is often ranked as one form of the civil freedom of association; but its intention and purpose are plainly economic. Watertight compartments, however, are the rule in ships, not in social affairs, where indeed they are quite exceptional. These leakages do not destroy the usefulness of classification; for merely to make such a classification brings out the fact that the effect of public economic planning upon, say, the freedom to ask for your cards and sweep out, is likely to be, at the least, more direct than its impact upon freedom from imprisonment without trial.

The language of the preceding sentence suggests a further distinction of which a good deal has sometimes been made: that is, the distinction between freedom "from" and freedom "to." Colonel Geoffrey Vickers has treated this as fundamental in his interesting, if rather sinister, paper on *Purpose and Force*.[4] "The conception that freedom means the unrestricted opportunity to move in any direction or to stand still, as caprice may dictate," he writes in the course of an attack upon J. S. Mill's concept of liberty, "is a modern and calamitous delusion, the falsity

4. Royal Institute of International Affairs, World Order Papers, pp. 51, 52.

of which can only be concealed by prosperity. A castaway on a desert island, hunting gull's eggs for his food, would not count his freedom from interference as liberty." On this view, freedom is said to have a "positive" quality: it becomes material to ask not "How much Freedom?" but "Freedom for whom and for what?" (This has a very dangerous sound: freedom is in danger when people begin to ask what you want it for.) A great gulf, it is suggested, lies between the negative conception of freedom as "freedom from interference," and positive freedom in the sense of "opportunity."

Nevertheless', I doubt if the difference between freedom "from" and freedom "to" amounts to much more than the habit of calling the freedoms that we already enjoy by one set of names, and those which we lack by another. If this country were to become subject to a Hitlerite gestapo, the vocal classes would sigh for freedom *from* spying and arbitrary arrest, just as the unemployed used to clamor for freedom *from* want. All freedoms are simultaneously freedom *to* do what you want, and freedom *from* whatever prevents you from doing this. The question whether emphasis is laid upon the obstacles, or upon the use to be made of the freedom, is a question which of the two, in the circumstances of the moment, happens to loom larger. It has nothing to do with the qualitative nature of different freedoms, or the purpose to which they are put. A hungry man is unlikely either to play a good game of football or to make an effective political organizer, and lack of money prevents a man equally from buying pamphlets and from buying drinks. But so does imprisonment.

The task is, then, to inquire how significant contemporary freedoms are likely to be affected by authoritative public choice of economic priorities. On this, extreme opinions are held. On the one hand we read (near the *beginning* of a book in a *discussion* series): "Public planning means that enterprise, labour, distribution must be strictly regulated. It means, therefore, that one's chance to choose one's occupation must be reduced, since the plan cannot possibly be worked unless enough labour is directed into the occupation where it is needed, regardless of whether enough people want to do that kind of work or not. . . . In the same way, hours, pay, conditions will have to be standardised. Strikes, as also lock-outs, must become illegal. . . . Ambitious people will not be at liberty to take chances with their careers unless the proper officials allow it (and officials are not commonly venturesome) . . . public authorities must obviously take a larger and larger part in cultural activities if these are not to be allowed to languish . . . teachers and teaching must be more or less standardised. . . ." [5]

These dogmatic statements do not seem to leave much room for discussion. In this case, however, one dogmatism is answered by another. Contrast the following:—

"A planned society can be a far more free society than the competitive *laissez-faire* order which it has come to replace. Its greater freedom lies in its ability to offer those who work in it the sense, on the one hand, of continuous opportunity for the expression of capacity, and the power, on the other, to share fully in making the rules under which they work. The failure of the pre-war order was the degree to which, in the daily economic life of the worker, it made freedom and security dependent on privi-

5. Muriel Jaeger, *Liberty versus Equality* (Nelson Discussion Series), pp. 11, ff.

lege. Men feel that a social order is just only when their hopes are not frustrated and their future not in constant danger: justice is the parent of freedom." [6] "The alternatives before us are stark. . . . There is no remedy now for our ills save, with all its complexities, the planned production of our economic resources for community consumption. . . . And it cannot be too strongly emphasised that those who seek the new social order are in this hour the soldiers of freedom. . . . A society like ours . . . is incapable of the security which, as this book has argued, is the basic condition of freedom. Not only so. The greater the effort to restore its security upon its present foundations, the greater the attack upon freedom that is involved." [7]

It was, I think, Bertrand Russell who remarked that, should the temperature of a room unhappily become the subject of political controversy, two political parties would hold two views—one would stand for boiling-point, the other for freezing.

It does not, however, follow that where strong opinions conflict the right answer is found by splitting the difference. That might be true of a dispute about temperature: it is not likely to be true in the freedom-under-planning controversy, except in a qualitative sense. The sensible answer is not that freedom is best promoted by a judiciously moderate dose of planning—something between that prescribed by Miss Jaeger and Professor Laski, respectively. The sensible answer turns on an analysis of the impact of planning upon different *kinds* of freedom.

6. The Labour Party, *The Old World and The New Society.*
7. Laski, *Liberty in The Modern State,* Pelican Edition, pp. 39, 40.

A limited plan might wholly destroy certain freedoms: while a plan of much more comprehensive scope might leave other freedoms quite untouched. Here it is clear that Miss Jaeger on the one side, and Professor Laski and the Labour Party on the other, are thinking about different kinds of freedom. Neither side denies that economic planning can fill the belly. The Left asserts that when the belly is full we are free from the necessity of filling it: the opposition replies that the price of filling it is the surrender of the freedom to use this freedom as we wish. Both *could* be right. If they are, the simultaneous enjoyment of economic, civil and political freedoms is impossible. That at least makes the problem important.

In the background of this controversy there lies one further distinction which is quite fundamental. That is the distinction between those effects on freedom which are inherent in any kind of plan, and those which are related to the content of a particular plan, or to the particular method of its operation. If Miss Jaeger is right and *any* plan is incompatible with the chief economic, political and civil freedoms, then the problems concerned with the differences between one plan and another are not worth discussing. We are sunk anyway. If, on the other hand the mere technique of planning is not necessarily destructive of these freedoms, it certainly does not follow that all the problems of freedom under planning are settled. To show, for instance, that the government can effectively determine economic priorities without recourse to compulsory direction of labor is not the same as to show that any actual economic plan will be either wise or popular or conducive to freedom. To show that planners need not exercise certain powers is not the same as to show that they will not. To show that it is possible to plan for good is not the same as to show that it is impossible to plan for evil.

To simplify the discussion, these two sets of problems are treated separately in the pages that follow. The first nine chapters of this book are concerned with those effects on freedom which may result from the fact of planning: to keep the issue clear, it is assumed throughout these chapters that the planners are public-spirited people who seek only to discover the common good, and to do their best for it. In the final chapter this assumption is challenged. Where and how, we then ask, can we find safeguards that the men and women who have the power to choose will in practice plan for, and not against, the freedom of those in whose name this power is exercised? Astonishingly little attention has been given to this second group of problems—and that in the age of Hitler, Mussolini, Mustapha Kemal and Stalin. The thinkers of the Right, satisfied with their demonstration of the inherent incompatibility of planning and freedom, can legitimately pass these problems by; but the common assumption of the Left that disproof of the inevitability of this contradiction is enough to establish the case for planning is too facile. "The essence of Democracy" says *Commonwealth,* "is that the resources of the State are a common possession to be managed on behalf of all, by the representatives of all, *for the benefit of all.*" [8] Before this essence can be distilled into concrete social and political institutions, however, a number of conditions must be fulfilled. The justification of planning, in terms of freedom, must be that by conscious collective decision of economic priorities our

8. *Commonwealth.* Five-Point Program, p. 9. Italics mine.

frustrations are diminished and our freedoms enlarged: that we have more opportunity to do what we want to do. This in turn implies (1) that objectives exist which can properly be described as "for the benefit of all," (2) that these objectives can be ascertained with reasonable accuracy, and (3) that the men and women on whom lies the duty of making decisions "for the benefit of all and on behalf of all" will in fact continuously pursue these objectives.

To illustrate these points:—it is not, to begin with, axiomatic that in every community some common good exists in the sense of ends which would be freely chosen by all members of that community. Thus, if three people wish to spend a holiday together, and one wants to go to Margate, one to Bath and one to Edinburgh, no planner can decide, on behalf of all, and according to the wishes of all, where the holiday is to be spent. If he claims to decide "for the benefit of all" he is necessarily importing into his decision some criterion of benefit other than the wishes of the parties. He may decide in favor of the person he likes best, the place he likes best, or the claim of that member of the trio who, in his judgment, has the best taste or the most urgent need of a holiday: or on any other principle. But in these circumstances no plan can "give the people what they want," as distinct from what somebody else thinks that they want, or ought to want. And conflicts of this kind are not confined to small groups, or to such comparatively trivial issues as those raised in this example.

The second condition—that the common good not only exists but can be known—may raise formidable difficulties in a large and complex society. To determine the complete schedule of economic preferences of, say, 30 million individuals, is a very different matter from ascertaining where three people wish to spend a holiday. Of recent years a good deal of attention has been paid to this problem by economists. I shall cheerfully suggest that it is in practice insoluble—in the sense that no technique exists, or can be devised, which will scientifically establish the correctness of any one answer. The uses which even 3 million people, let alone 30 or 300 million, can make of their time, energy and resources are, practically speaking, infinitely variable. The statement that the problem of determining, in an exact quantitative sense, the ideal pattern of production for any community is scientifically insoluble, simply means that there is no way of proving that the members of that community might not have preferred some other pattern, different, in certain particulars, from that which was, in fact, planned, or which was, in fact, realized in the absence of any plan. More excursion trains and fewer charabancs, or a pub on the corner instead of a cinema—who knows whether these might not be judged improvements on things as they are? To admit, however, that the problem is insoluble is no cause for despair, nor for the abdication of judgment. Exact mathematical solutions of significant human problems are indeed seldom possible. Yet we recognize that it is possible, by taking thought, to arrive at recognizably better answers than those reached by the wholly thoughtless. To take one obvious parallel: the most happily married man cannot be sure that there is not somewhere in the world a woman with whom he would not have lived in even greater happiness than with his present spouse. In this sense the problem of finding the ideal wife is insoluble in exactly the same way as the problem of determining the ideal pattern of economic priorities for any community. In neither case can you be *certain* that you might not have done better. It does not follow that you should either marry without a moment's reflection, or abandon economic planning in despair.

Granted that some common needs exist and that these can be, if not known, at least the subject of better or worse guesses, freedom still demands assurance that it is for these needs and no others that the planners shall in fact plan. This is probably the most tricky part of the whole business; for the observed behavior of human beings in positions of power hardly justifies an easy assumption that they will automatically act, according to the best of their ability and understanding, "on behalf of all and for the benefit of all." The fact that this assumption is so generally, and so light-heartedly, made by those who are convinced of the beneficial potentialities of planning is no doubt a tribute to the good hearts of those who make it. They generously ascribe to others their own good intentions, picturing all planners as men and women as zealous and public-spirited as they are themselves. It is a generous optimism: but the prudent will not forget the fact that planning is not possible without power, and that power, whether in the hands of prime minister or railway guard, is potential tyranny. A wise choice of planners and a watchful eye on plans may well be the price of freedom.

None of these three conditions, as I hope to suggest in the pages that follow, is incapable of fulfillment. But they will not fulfill themselves.

CHAPTER II

Cultural and Civil Freedoms

I

IN THE background of any discussion of the compatibility of economic planning and cultural freedom, there lurks a fundamental philosophic issue. Is it in fact possible to plan for indeterminate cultural ends? For real cultural freedom demands not merely variety, but actual indeterminacy, of cultural ends. Such freedom is not achieved, unless economic planning sets people free to do and say things of their own choosing—things which are not known beforehand to, much less decided by, the planners. That would imply a fundamental difference between the political state and all other forms of association which involve organized action. The political state, where there is real cultural freedom, is no more than a convenient instrument for promoting the joint and several purposes of its members, and has no specific, determinate purpose of its own beyond this. A trade union exists to create better conditions of employment for its members, a church to promote the worship of God, a dramatic society to produce, if not to appreciate, drama; but the state exists—for what? To make it possible for men and women to live their own lives in their own way.

In the past, however, these states—groups of human

beings organized politically in geographical units—have, on the one hand, found a determinate purpose in the defense of each against armed aggression by the others (or in the conduct of such armed aggression) and in activities incidental to this purpose, such as the cultivation of an imperialist and martial spirit; while, on the other hand, they have been content in large measure to leave other social ends to look after themselves. Things are changing, however, in more ways than one. In the first place, civilized people do not now take pride and pleasure in warfare, and find it increasingly difficult to defend military prowess as the proper and primary social purpose of political groups. In the second place, as our way of life grows more complicated, individuals within the state find it increasingly difficult to pursue their own ends satisfactorily without a great deal of help from the state itself. The second change leads to a demand for state planning; while the first creates a vacuum in the place of some determinate end for which to plan.

The right way to meet this situation is not, I think, to cast about for some new social purpose with which to fill that vacuum. It is certainly tempting to do so, and many of the attempts to achieve integration through religious revivals or quasi religious syntheses [1] (when they have

1. A good example is to be found in Mr. J. B. Coates' book *A Common Faith.** Mr. Coates seems to have got into a proper muddle. On p. 53 he believes that "the liberal *states* will find themselves obliged, by the necessities of the objective situation if by no other reason, to *plan the cultural* and *psychological* as well as the political and economic aspects of their *national* life." They will in consequence "need to bring under a unified control the two functions performed in the past by Church and state." I take this to mean that the liberal state will have to adopt a definite system of moral and cultural values—the "new synthesis" which Mr. Coates

any concrete meaning at all) are illustrations of the force
of this temptation. Nevertheless this is, I submit, the wrong
end at which to begin. It is wrong because of the two
peculiarities which distinguish the state from all other
forms of association—the fact that membership is compulsory, and the fact that the rules made by the state are
backed up by physical force. An association with both
these peculiarities cannot, by definition, both respect cultural freedom and pursue specific cultural ends. It cannot
do both these things because minorities who reject these
ends can neither defy the law nor resign their membership of the state by which that law is enforced: they therefore lose their cultural freedom. For instance, if Parliament
should decide that the proper cultural purpose of this
country is to exalt the Christian religion and to exterminate
atheistic practices, it would be necessary to suppress all
agnostic societies and publications, and to take steps to see
that every child was taught the Christian doctrine and that
every adult took his part in Christian worship. This is
not cultural freedom for non-Christians. (If in the two
preceding sentences the word "Marxist" is substituted for
"Christian" we have a scarcely exaggerated description

---

is concerned to create in our divided societies. But on p. 55 we read
"The danger of the wrong kind of social control being set up over
the minds of men everywhere is a very grave one, for *a cultural
synthesis imposed by the state* will always tend to be contrary to
man's truest insight." (Italics mine throughout.)

Which is it to be? We cannot have it both ways. Either the state,
which is a force-controlling organization, imposes a synthesis (in the
sense of a system of moral and cultural values) or it doesn't. If it
does, there is no cultural freedom. Mr. Coates and all the would-be
democrats who sigh after the glories of totalitarian achievement
overlook the fundamental distinction that while conformity can be
imposed, agreement cannot.

* London: George Allen & Unwin Ltd.

of the policy of the Soviet government in the early years of the revolution.) There is, moreover, no parallel to this power in any form of association other than the political state; for no other society which adopted policies or principles of which even a minority of its members disapproved could prevent those members from resigning their membership, or compel their compliance by law. I think it is still true in this country, though not perhaps as securely true as might be wished, that this incompatibility of freedom with the pursuit of specific ends by the political state is appreciated, so far as religious freedom is concerned. The power of the state is not therefore used, as it was for instance used at one time in Russia, to compel compliance with official doctrine. What we have to do is to accept this as a *general* truth, applicable to cultural freedoms *generally*. Voluntary societies can and should commit themselves to specific cultural ends: compulsory societies should not.

The problem of planning for freedom thus resolves itself into the problem of determinate planning for indeterminate cultural ends. Stated thus it sounds insoluble. Once again, however, a problem which is theoretically insoluble in the limiting case, turns out to be quite tractable in the concrete form in which it is likely to crop up in practice. We need not despair of the possibility of combining useful planning and cultural freedom, provided that certain conditions are observed.

The first condition is the obvious one that such planning must know where to stop. There are few, if any, cultural freedoms which can be enjoyed in such a vacuum that their exercise makes no demands whatever on the productive resources of the community. It follows that determination of economic priorities, carried to the ultimate limit, would prohibit cultural freedom. Freedom of speech, for example, is not the same thing as freedom of soliloquy. If speech is to be more than soliloquy, there must be an audience to hear what is said, or read what is written. That means a building in which an audience can be gathered, or a microphone to reach them in their own homes, or paper on which to write what they can read. Similarly, even the most austere forms of religious worship usually require a building in which they may be conducted, while many rituals demand organs, books, censers, candles, altar cloths. It follows that any government with absolute power to plan the use of the community's resources down to the last detail can make *effective* freedom of speech or of worship impossible for any body, person, or society, of whom it disapproves, merely by withholding such essential materials.

"Can," however, in this context is not, and must not be, the same word as "will." Admittedly it is possible for a state authority responsible for planning the output of the building industry to assign halls to the League of the Godless and to refuse them to the churches; or vice versa. But it is equally possible to make suitable buildings available for all denominations on the same terms. As Dr. Mannheim has remarked, it is possible to "co-ordinate the time tables of the different railway lines without controlling the topics of conversation inside the carriages.[2]

No one can lay down, in general terms, the exact limitation on the scope of economic planning which the preservation of cultural freedom demands. But the examples just given illustrate the kind of distinction which would

2. *Diagnosis of Our Time*, p. 103.

need to be drawn in practice; and they serve to show the fallacy of the assumption that extensive economic planning is *inherently* synonymous with uncompromising cultural conformity. As a matter of fact, the policy of the Soviet Union in regard to religious freedom has actually undergone important changes since the early days of the revolution. Religious freedom has been increased without relaxation of state determination of economic priorities. This at least proves that alternative courses are possible.

It is therefore not enough for Professor Hayek to assert (quite correctly) that "the power of the planner over our private lives" rests on his power over production.[3] It does. But power can be exercised in different ways and in different degrees. All extensions of power involve certain risks: some offer advantages also. If the advantages did not sometimes outweigh the risks, complete anarchy would be preferable to any government. In any particular instance it is necessary to weigh the risks against the possible advantages and to decide in the light of this balance. The argument is not advanced by prejudging the issue in favor of the risks. To condemn all economic planning on the ground that if carried to extremes it *can* be used to nullify all freedom of expression is of a piece with forbidding innocent activities on the ground that in certain circumstances they would be anti-social. I have heard it argued, for example, that it is, in all circumstances, wrong to play tennis or golf on Sundays, since, in certain conditions, to do so might disturb a neighbor's devotions, or deprive the caddy of his Sabbath rest. It would be safer to say that Sunday games are wrong because they offend against

3. Friedrich A. Hayek, *The Road to Serfdom* (London, George Routledge & Sons; Chicago, The University of Chicago Press, 1944), p. 93. (Page numbers refer to the American edition.)

the will of God: for this argument has at least the advantage of being incapable of disproof. In terms of any rational utilitarian ethic, these all-or-nothing arguments are equally indefensible, whether applied to economic planning or to Sabbatarian principles.

Somewhat similar is the argument which contends that cultural freedom and economic planning are incompatible since an economic plan and a cultural pattern are, for practical purposes, identical. If the term "cultural" is defined sufficiently widely, this is certainly true in part; but there is no reason why it should be wholly true, unless we perversely wish to make it so. Moreover, the points at which cultural freedom is unavoidably restricted by an economic plan are also the points at which it would be restricted in the absence of any such plan. If cultural liberty means individual freedom to determine the whole way of life, we are bound to admit that this freedom must be in great measure foregone in any large and complex society. An example should make the point clear. The size of cities has an important influence on the average citizen's ability to spend life as he pleases. In very large cities (arranged as such cities are now) it is, to mention only one thing, necessary for many to spend much time in traveling. But if you happen to be one of those who wish, say, that London were a smaller city, you are individually powerless to bring this about. You *may* be able to go and live in a smaller place, Letchworth for example: but living in Letchworth is not the same thing as living in a smaller London. The degree of urbanization of the community, with all the limitations on one's personal freedom which that implies, has for practical purposes to be accepted by the ordinary individual.

It is important, however, to repeat that this restriction has nothing to do with economic planning. The size and shape of most of our present cities are, at present, only in a very small degree the result of the conscious determination of economic priorities. London and Liverpool have not been made: they have happened. But the individual is not, on that account, the more able to modify them to suit his own taste. All that he can do to that end is himself to live outside their boundaries. In that way, by lowering the demand for urban accommodation he casts his vote, for what it is worth (in what Professor Mises has called the ballot box of the market place), against the growth of cities. But it is at best a vote in a very large and undemocratic constituency. Similarly, in cases where the size of towns is consciously determined as a matter of deliberate policy he can, in a democratic society, exercise some tiny weight of opinion. It is a matter for argument, in the light of the particular circumstances of particular cases, whether planning increases or diminishes the freedom of the individual to shape his own cultural pattern in such matters as this. Whichever way the argument goes, however, two things are clear. First, so long as we live in large and complex communities, this freedom is unavoidably very narrowly restricted, whatever method is used for determining economic priorities. And second, none of this alters the fact that there is a world of difference between a society in which people are allowed to say what they please and one in which they are not, even though the externals of life in both cases may be much the same, people living in the same sort of cities and following even much the same daily routine. Moscow, Berlin, New York, Mexico City and London begin to look remarkably alike: the quality of life to be lived in each of them remains different.

It is, therefore, nonsense to assert that comprehensive economic planning *cannot* stop short of the point at which it destroys all cultural freedom. The critical issue is this business of knowing where to stop. While, as has been said, there can be no general answer to this question, there are one or two things that are worth remembering in this context. For instance, the temptation to exact unnecessary cultural uniformity is always likely to be strong amongst those men and women who are personally responsible for making the decisions which constitute economic planning. It will be strong because it is, generally speaking, easier to plan for uniformity than for diversity. It will be strong because people who arrive at positions of power are, inevitably, people who enjoy the exercise of power. This is, of course, as true of the powerful whose intentions are good as of those whose designs are evil. Both are likely to find it more satisfying that people should do what those in authority want them to do or think that they should do, rather than what they themselves want to do.

In practice this means that the lengths to which economic planning can safely be carried depend on a number of intangibles such as the quality of the planners (a matter to be dealt with in Chapter X), and the general social conditions of the community in which it is conducted. The critical fields are those of the press, broadcasting, education and any other powerful determinants of public opinion. In the case of education, for example, British and Scandinavian experience at least has already demonstrated that a considerable degree of cultural diversity is possible within a system in which most of the schools are owned, and the teachers paid, by public bodies. The same experience has also shown that this freedom has its limits; but there is no reason to suppose that these limits are fixed for all time, and they are certainly not the same in all countries. It is in the light of considerations like this that one must decide on merits in each instance whether it is expedient to retain a privately-owned press, privately-owned schools, or to permit a public monopoly in broadcasting. These are not so much questions of principle as of expediency. They are also specialist questions which need much fuller discussion than I can give them here. I would only hazard the opinions that it is doubtful whether the time has come in this country when educational freedom is sufficiently secure for a complete state monopoly (which would involve, among other things, the abolition or transfer to public ownership of all the present "progressive schools") to be enthusiastically advocated; and that the evils of a privately-owned press could be greatly diminished by control of profits and advertising revenue.

The second condition of successful economic planning for indeterminate cultural ends is that the planners should show a nice discrimination in their methods. There has been some muddled thinking here amongst democrats who have wistfully observed the success of totalitarian regimes in putting over totalitarian ideologies; and who long to enlist some of the same techniques in the cause of democracy. The answer is that many of these techniques are simply not applicable to the promotion of indeterminate ends. The hysterical dramatization of politics, in which the Nazis have specialized, is a terrifyingly powerful instrument for the creation of a mass mind bent on uniformity. Similar methods cannot, in the nature of things, be employed in the service of diversity and freedom. The progressive political parties in this country seem to be in a great state of conflict about all this. Covetous of the success of their enemies, they are tempted to dabble in emotional propaganda appealing to motives that are both irrational and irrelevant to the issues to be decided. Their experiments in this field range from the use of party colors to well-staged processions and pageants. On the whole, however, the Left, in this country, does these things badly. It does them badly because it does them half-heartedly; and it is half-hearted because it is more than half aware of their fundamental incompatibility with the very freedoms in whose cause they are enlisted. This, and not only lack of money, is the reason why the Left in this country is generally speaking less efficient at this sort of game than the Right. Irrational propaganda can, within limits, be used to create opinion in favor of ends chosen by the propagandists: it cannot, in the nature of things, be successful in the service of ends to be selected by those to whom the propaganda is directed. The nineteenth-century thinkers, whom it is now fashionable to decry, were consistent and right in their assumption that political democracy implies a rational approach to politics. They were wrong only in exaggerating the actual rationalism of the actual electorate. If it should unhappily prove true that men and women generally cannot ever attain the degree of rationality which political democracy demands, the answer would not be that an up-to-date democracy should treat them as the irrational creatures that they are. The answer would be that a free democratic society is impossible. There are no short cuts to freedom.

II

Of all our liberties those that are least likely to be threatened by economic planning are the civil rights concerned with the method of enforcement of the law, and the position of the actual or supposed lawbreaker. Even Professor Hayek does not specifically suggest that these are in danger. Of course any large extension of the functions of government necessarily multiplies the number of possible offenses against laws and regulations. Everybody is well aware of this from war-time experience: indeed there must be few, even of the most conscientious citizens, who have not, advertently or inadvertently, been guilty of breaking some war-time regulation. This multiplication of the possible occasions of offense is, however, a quite different matter from the procedure adopted to ensure that the law is kept, or the methods of dealing with offenders. There is no logical connection between state regulation of the output of mining or agriculture or any or all industries on the one hand, and the abolition of *habeas corpus* or of trial by jury, or the establishment of a gestapo, on the other. Here again, war-time experience in Britain is, on the whole, comforting. It is true that a serious breach in these civil rights has been made by the Home Secretary's power under Defense Regulation 18b to imprison without charge or trial persons who, in his personal opinion, ought to be incarcerated: but it is also true, both that this power has been sparingly exercised, and that in the stresses of war there may be occasions for suspicion which have nothing whatever to do with state control of economic priorities. I am not arguing that, even so, the public safety might not have been adequately safeguarded without use of these powers. But even the undoubted wrong inflicted on a certain number of entirely harmless and innocent individuals does not alter the fact that such treatment is still quite exceptional. The vast bulk of offenses against all the new, as well as the old, laws are dealt with through the ordinary courts and with such protections as these afford. These protections are not perhaps in practice in every case as complete as they appear on paper. Nevertheless they are real. Under our present war-time laws a man can be imprisoned for inciting others to strike (outside a Trade Union meeting), for bad timekeeping on essential work, or for dealing on the black market. For these and for the hundreds of other offenses like them the machinery of 18b is not employed, any more than it is used for dealing with thieves and motoring offenders or persons suspected of other pre-war crimes. And it is still true in this country that a man cannot disappear overnight, without any charge being preferred against him, and never be heard of again. Words like totalitarian and Fascism are loosely used: such use should not be allowed to obscure the fact that we are not, in this sense, totalitarian. And we have established as a matter of experienced fact that, even under the stresses of war, comprehensive economic planning is possible without recourse to such totalitarianisms.

This experience is the more remarkable since the multiplication of offenses due to economic planning, or to other war-time exigencies (such as blackout) creates an undoubted temptation to short-circuit the slow and cumbrous methods of British justice. A certain amount of nibbling at the edges of civil freedom has certainly taken place as a result of this temptation. It has, for instance, been argued that witnesses who may be engaged on war work ought not to be brought to court in cases where it is anticipated that a plea of guilty will probably make their attendance unnecessary. This means that if, in fact, a plea of not guilty is entered, a case must be adjourned for these witnesses to be called. The mere fact that such an adjournment will be necessary is in itself an inducement to many defendants to plead guilty; when you are before the courts (especially on charges that are not very serious) the desire to be over and done with it often prevails over everything else. This is certainly a danger with young people; and the practice in some juvenile courts of not calling witnesses for the prosecution at a first hearing in war-time has been a matter of concern to magistrates. Such modifications of judicial practice are a warning; but not more. Police and other public officials are always open to temptation to save their own time and trouble at the expense of other people's freedom. A part, though by no means all, of the law's delays are justified as safeguards against this temptation. If economic planning increases the pressure on the courts, as it well may, the remedy is twofold. First, we should provide judicial machinery adequate to meet any demands made upon it without sacrificing the established defenses of freedom; and, second, we should watch and, if necessary, strengthen those defenses. The inference here from war to peace conditions is, as often, invalid for the reason that in war the value of time is disproportionately high.

State economic planning does not, in short, alter the fact that power will be used by cruel and tyrannous people in one way, and by the humane and the lovers of liberty in another. We are thus brought back to the

distinction between "can" and "will." Just as the power
of the state *can* be used to destroy all cultural freedom,
so also it *can* be directed against every kind of civil
freedom. Whether it *will* be used in either or both of
these ways depends on how far political power is in practice absolute, and what kind of people exercise that power
for what kind of ends. The judicial species of civil freedom
in particular—that is, fundamentally, freedom from arbitrary punishment—is only *necessarily* threatened by economic planning if it is true that a government which takes
responsibility for economic decisions is for some reason
necessarily composed of more dictatorial people than one
which leaves these matters alone. In a chapter which carries the question-begging title: *Why the Worst Get on Top,*
Professor Hayek has attempted to establish that this is
probable. Since this is essentially a question of the quality
of plans and planners his argument is dealt with in Chapter X.[4]

The whole question of the impact of economic planning upon both cultural and civil freedoms has been
greatly confused by ill-considered inferences from the
experience of the U.S.S.R. That country offers the one
and only example of really comprehensive economic planning in time of peace which the world has yet seen.
Throughout this experiment the degree of both civil and
cultural freedom permitted to Soviet citizens has been

4. Of course if Professor Hayek's thesis is right, this distinction
between the technique of planning and the contents of particular
plans loses all significance. If all plans are necessarily made by bad
people for bad ends, then any discussion of the impact of good
plans upon personal freedoms must be ludicrously academic. In
other words the first nine chapters of this book become irrelevant,
and Chapter X wrong.

intolerably low by the standards which the British up-
hold for themselves (though not everywhere for their
Empire). The Soviet plans, have, however, from the beginning, been avowedly devoted to promotion of specific
cultural ends: first, the promulgation of Marxist-Leninist
doctrine, then, in later years, the increase in the military
strength and prestige of the Soviet people. There have
indeed been changes from time to time: the expulsion of
Trotsky from the ranks of the elect, for instance, involved
certain revisions in official doctrine. Down to 1927 the
Soviet citizen was free to speak of Trotsky in terms of
the highest admiration, but enjoyed no corresponding
freedom to denounce him: after that date these freedoms
and unfreedoms changed places. Again, there have been
changes, to which reference has already been made, in
the degree of religious freedom permitted. There seems
also to have been a decided shift of emphasis, no doubt
associated with the growing importance attached to military considerations, away from traditional socialist inter-
nationalism towards a much more conventional type of
nationalistic patriotism. But throughout the twenty-seven
years since the revolution there have always been plenty
of opinions which no Soviet citizen could safely express.
The retort commonly offered by fanatical Soviet admirers,
that no Soviet citizen ever wishes to say anything but
what the law permits, is a poor defense either of freedom
or of the Soviet authorities. It is clear that up till now
the Soviet government does not conceive its task as a
matter of economic planning for indeterminate ends. That
being so, one cannot reasonably expect that Soviet experience will throw any great light on the practicability of
such a project.

As for civil liberties, let us remember the background. The Soviet system was begotten and born in the violence of revolution and civil war. It was the child, on the one side, of the Czarist Empire, and on the other of an expressly anti-democratic Marxist policy. In a country accustomed to secret police, political imprisonment and assassination, the new government openly set out to establish a particular type of dictatorship. In these conditions, civil liberties, as we understand them, could not be destroyed by the revolution, since they were not there to destroy. Between the introduction of the revised constitution of 1936 and the German invasion of Russia there was indeed a good deal of talk about relaxation of some of the rigors of the dictatorship, especially in the direction of greater political freedom. No one, however, who reads the Soviet authorities' own enthusiastic accounts of the work of their political prisoners, or who has personally known men and women whose relatives disappeared overnight in the great purges, or who has read press summaries of the Moscow trials of the nineteen-thirties, with their fervent denunciations of the treachery of defendants whose cases were still *sub judice*—no one who has given a moment's attention to any of this evidence can pretend that the Soviet range of civil liberties is comparable with that to which we are accustomed in this country. Equally, however, in the light of the declared objectives of the Soviet government, no one can conclude in the light of this experience that the attempt to combine civil liberty and economic planning has been tried and has failed.

Inferences from the Soviet experiment are likely to crop up repeatedly, whatever the particular liberties that may be under discussion. Just as the Soviet plans have been carried out against a certain civil and cultural background, so also their execution has made use of certain economic compulsions, or restrictions on economic liberties which are highly prized elsewhere. It may be useful, therefore, to summarize here what would appear in every case to be the limits of safe inference from Russian practice. In the first place, Soviet experience can be illuminating when there have from time to time been changes in the quantity or quality of liberty allowed under that regime. In such cases we learn, at the least, that it is *possible* to do things in more ways than one, and we may, in addition, have material for instructive comparisons. Second, Soviet experience is useful in so far as it gives positive evidence of the compatibility of planning with particular freedoms. Positive evidence proves that a thing can be done: negative evidence not that it cannot, but that it has not. Thus positive evidence from the U.S.S.R. has established that it is possible to plan at least up to the Soviet level of efficiency in time of peace without recourse to universal industrial conscription. Negative evidence, such as the fact that there are no legal opposition parties in the U.S.S.R., proves nothing except that there are no legal opposition parties in the U.S.S.R.

CHAPTER III

The Freedom of the Consumer

I. FREEDOM TO SPEND

T HE DIVISION between consumer and producer is not, of course, except in a small number of cases, a division between separate classes of persons; it is, as a rule, a distinction between different aspects, or different interests, of the same person. But the statement that we are nearly all both producers and consumers (though true) does not justify dismissing the distinction as of no practical importance. During the greater part of active adult life, most people are producers of some one or two articles or services for something like eight hours a day: during the whole twenty-four hours they are consumers of a great variety of articles or services, both while at work, and also throughout childhood, after retirement, and in periods of incapacity. Even when asleep in bed, we are wearing out the bedclothes. It follows that (quite apart from certain risks of losing on the swings of consumption what is gained upon the productive roundabouts, which are discussed later) [1] freedom of consumption is immensely important, because it does literally affect every minute of our lives. It is indeed a theoretical platitude that the satisfaction of the needs of the consumer is the

1. See pp. 55 ff.

essential purpose and justification of productive activity: though, to judge from the way in which the world is organized, one might hardly have thought so.

Freedom of consumption means freedom to get what you like when you like. One is tempted also to add freedom to get as much as you like. Since, however, the total amount of a person's consumption is generally, in practice, settled in the light of his activities or status as a producer, it will be convenient for the time being to regard the total quantity of each individual's consumption as fixed, and to concern ourselves only with the range of freedom for choice within this total. It will also be convenient to reserve for later discussion some fascinating, but tricky, problems which arise if the consumer enjoys freedom to distribute a given total as he likes through time—*i.e.*, freedom to consume *when* he likes.

In this and most other economically developed countries before the war, we should commonly have described freedom of consumption as freedom to "spend our *money* as we like." This phrase is capable, however, of bearing two fundamentally different meanings. First, it may simply mean freedom to distribute a given sum of money in any way that the owner likes amongst all the things that are available for him to buy. Even in time of war, and still more, of course, in the unrestricted markets of peace, a pound in your pocket can be converted into an almost infinite variety of different objects in your house, on your person, in your stomach, or for use in other ways. Used in this way, the phrase "freedom of consumption" takes the productive pattern, so to speak, for granted. In its second meaning, however, this phrase implies a claim that the choices which consumers do actually make should continuously determine this pattern of production. It is an assertion of what has been called "consumers' sovereignty." The second is a much more subtle and sophisticated interpretation of freedom of consumption than the first, and it probably goes a good deal further than what most people mean when they express the wish to spend their money as they please. Full consumers' sovereignty in this sense is, however, definitely not compatible with economic planning as we have defined it. It is not possible for the *same* questions to be settled *both* by the conscious and deliberate decisions of planners, *and* as the unconscious, unforeseen, results of the behavior of millions of consumers acting independently of one another. The planners could of course carefully watch the market and take account of the fads and fancies of consumers there revealed: if they had sense in their heads, they would certainly include this evidence in the material upon which their decisions were based. But if they carried this attention to consumer behavior to such lengths that the final result of planning was just to copy as accurately as possible the picture that would result if no plan were made, the planners would in fact have ceased to plan. Planned decisions and unplanned market reactions are in fact *alternative* ways of determining economic priorities. Use can be made of both in different parts of the economic field (*e.g.*, the output of saucepans can be planned and that of penny-whistles left to the market), but in the determination of any particular issue they are mutually exclusive. The case for planning is not that it is identical with, but that, in certain circumstances, it is superior to, the planless method of settling economic priorities.

Whether the incompatibility of consumer sovereignty,

in this second sense, with economic planning is or is not a serious infringement of freedom is discussed in the next chapter. We may now come back to the simpler concept of freedom of consumption which implies no more than the liberty of every individual to choose in what shape he will take out his share of the good things which, by one or other method, are provided for the satisfaction of the public's needs. Even this, of course, must in all cases be subject to the limitation that the total of what is consumed by all, must, broadly speaking, keep in step with the total of what is produced for all (on whatever principle of priority). People in the aggregate cannot at any one moment consume more stuff than exists at that moment; and if they fail to use what has in fact been produced, time and materials will have been wasted in the making of that which is left unused. The problem involved in freedom of consumption is thus to allow the maximum of choice within the available total to each individual or group of individuals, while at the same time making sure that all these choices add up to the right total.

In this context, the popular expression "freedom to spend one's *money* as one likes," is useful as a reminder that the use of money (which, for all its possible abuses, is one of the greatest of civilizing inventions) secures virtually the maximum possible freedom of consumption. Money in one's pocket is an almost completely fluid form of consumption since it is, in time of peace, convertible into practically anything that can be made or done. From the point of view of freedom of consumption, the only improvement on the custom of using money would be a system in which, as in William Morris' *News from Nowhere,* everybody could take as much of everything as he wished without any kind of check whatever—*i.e.*, a condition in which there was no quantitative or qualitative check on consumption. This, however, is not on the map as a general method of distribution, at least not for any measurable time ahead. As an occasional method of distributing particular things, it is in use already side by side with money. The modern consumer in this country can both spend his money income as he wishes, and add to the enjoyments thus purchased as much consumption of the public roadways and parks and (in most districts) of the water laid on to his house, as he chooses. But, of course, in present circumstances, even apart from war, such unrationed free distribution is, the world over, an embroidery on the main fabric of consumption rather than the substance of the fabric itself.

In this matter, as so often in social affairs, the whole issue is quantitative. For practical purposes, distribution of commodities through money, supplemented by free distribution without limitation in particular cases, gives the maximum freedom of consumption. At the other end of the scale, compulsion to take what is given you up to the permitted amount, not in money but in kind, would abolish such freedom altogether. Between these extremes are a number of stages, all of which involve the use of what may be called different kinds of partial money. During the war, a great deal of ingenuity has been devoted to elaborating these half-in-half alternatives to money. In order to see clearly how far the use of the various possible methods of regulating consumption is compatible with economic planning, we may range the devices, other than money proper, that are already familiar to the British public in order of the freedom which they allow.

First comes the use of "points" (generally in conjunction with ordinary money). Points are themselves merely a subsidiary form of money, giving slightly less freedom of consumption than ordinary money. As used in this country they differ from ordinary money in four respects, the first two of which affect freedom of consumption. First, points are available only for the purchase of a limited and specified range of objects: they are, to this extent, money in their own little world of spam and rice, but, unlike real money, have no power outside that world. Second, points have only a restricted validity in time: they die within a month, whilst real money is as good as immortal. Third, points, which, like money proper, bestow a definite power of consumption on the consumer to whom they are assigned, confer no corresponding addition to the consuming power of the seller to whom they are transferred by this consumer. This distinction is of some interest, since it seriously affects the public attitude towards the manner in which both money and points manage the task, already mentioned, of matching total consumption with total available supply. In each case the method used demands that, as an article becomes scarcer, its value (in money or points as the case may be) should be raised, so that people will generally buy it less freely. This is necessary to prevent supplies from running out altogether. When money is used in this way, the greatest indignation is often expressed by the public; for an incidental by-product of this particular machinery for keeping the totals in step is an increase in the receipts, without any corresponding increase in the outgoings, of the sellers of articles which are running short. This is furiously denounced as profiteering. The use of money to give maximum freedom of individual consumption is thus necessarily open to the objection that it involves lining the pockets of the man whose shelves are stocked with goods that are becoming difficult to procure, and emptying the pockets of the man whose wares have outstripped demand.

People do not, on the other hand, feel at all the same about changes in points value necessary to limit demand where supplies are running short. A high point value is accepted without complaint where a high money price would be denounced, just because the high point value does not, and the high money value does, swell the shop-keeper's profit. We can, in fact, put up with going short, or having to make great sacrifices to get something we specially want, provided that we do not suspect that somebody else is making something out of the shortage. No doubt this attitude is strengthened also by the fact, which is the last of the four differences between points and money, that points are in practice distributed equally to all, subject only to certain minor differences which are explicitly defended on grounds of need. This last difference is not, it should be noted, in any sense an inherent distinction between points and money. It would be perfectly possible to distribute points (in the sense of money which can only be used once, and is available only for the purchase of a limited range of goods in a limited period of time) on any kind of principle that anybody cares to invent. It would also be possible to distribute money-proper equally to everybody. Money is money in fact in the full sense, and points are near-money, no matter who has how much of either of them.

After money and points come rations proper. These take us one step further away from freedom of consump-

tion. A rationing system, as distinct from distribution by
points, assigns a definite quantity of a specific commodity
to each consumer. Again, this quantity need not be the
same for all, although, in the case of foodstuffs, the scheme
is generally based on a sort of fundamental equality from
which particular departures are then justified on merits.
In so far, however, as rations have themselves to be
bought with ordinary money, a certain freedom of choice
within a given total still remains. If you have a pound to
spend each week, you cannot, at the time of writing, buy
more than two ounces of butter with it, nor could you do
so if instead of just one pound you had twenty or thirty.
If, however, you choose to go without your butter ration
you can buy a 2½d. stamp, which other people with similar incomes who faithfully consume their little dish of
butter must forego. This particular rationing system does
not, therefore, restrict the variety of consumption, except
by fixing a limit to each person's consumption of the rationed articles. The practice of selling rationed goods for
money implies, of course, that there are still unrationed
articles on the market on which that money could alternatively be spent. If this were not the case, there would
be no purpose in charging money prices for rations: they
might just as well be given away free.[2]

With a complete system of specific rationing of everything that is produced, we reach the final abolition of all
freedom of choice in consumption. Theoretically perhaps,
we could even then cherish on paper the right at least to
go without such part of our rations as we prefer to dis-
pense with: but in practice this would certainly prove to

2. This argument appears more pertinent in England, where the
wartime controls have been more comprehensive and rigorous than
in the United States.—*Publisher's note.*

be an empty academic kind of freedom if we could buy nothing else instead. The range of freedom of consumption possible under different methods of regulating distribution thus extends from virtually absolute freedom to no freedom at all, with a number of possible halting-places scattered between these extremes.

Every one of these methods is at least as consistent with a consciously planned determination of economic priorities as it is with a system that is left to plan itself. It is true that the complete aboltion of freedom of choice in consumption would probably prove unworkable under any system other than one which is comprehensively planned. But the converse of this proposition is unquestionably untrue. Planned production is certainly compatible with the method of distribution by money which, as we have seen, gives maximum freedom. Technically, the task of matching the total of goods already produced to the total claims upon those goods (as distinct from the task of adapting the future supply) is exactly the same, no matter what method of controlling production is employed. Once an article is there, it is too late to ask whether its production was or was not a mistake; though the answer to that question should naturally have a bearing on the issue whether the scale of production of similar articles in future should be expanded or contracted. Once a thing has been produced, the only question strictly relevant to that particular thing is the question who is to have it; and the possible answers to that question are unaffected by further inquiries as to how it came to be there in the first place. This is true, moreover, even though production and consumption are continuous processes, and though no sharp line separates the things that are here to be consumed today from those that still lie in the womb of tomorrow.

We thus reach the conclusion that the conscious planning of economic priorities involves no necessary threat to freedom of consumption in the sense in which we have so far used that phrase. Planned production can be distributed so as to allow as much liberty of personal choice as we have ever known; or it can be distributed in the most authoritarian fashion, as in an army, so as to allow no freedom of consumption at all. The most that can be said is that authoritarian methods are possibly less trouble to people in authority than are the more liberal alternatives. Even this, however, is not certain; and we must not succumb to the pessimism that assumes that people in official positions must always be anxious *and able* to insist that everything should be done in the way that gives least trouble to themselves. Indeed, to judge from some of the circuitous ways affected by some government departments, it would not seem that public officials even invariably wish to make such a demand, let alone succeed in carrying it.

This is one of the issues on which Soviet experience has something positive to say. The Russians in the early days of the revolution, and before they had set about economic planning in earnest, experimented lavishly with completely free distribution. The results were quite chaotic at that stage. Next, they receded into a strict system of rationing which covered all the principal foodstuffs, as well as many other articles; supplementing this by an unbelievably complicated system of selling the same things to different people at different prices, as well as allowing additional unrationed supplies of rationed articles to be sold on the open market at prices much higher than those charged for rationed supplies. This lasted through the early years of comprehensive planning, until in 1936 rationing was wholly abolished (until the war), along with differential systems of pricing the same articles. Thereafter, with the exception of certain free public services (like the health and education services which are also supplied *gratis* in other countries without a revolution) consumables generally were offered for sale in shops at fixed prices to anybody who cared to spend his money on buying them. The Soviet citizen then reached the stage of being able to "spend his money as he liked." But the government planning of production priorities went on as before.

Freedom of consumption is, of course, in all cases conditional upon the rules of the game being observed. In so far as we continue to enjoy the freedom of being paid not in kind but in money, the prices of goods offered for sale must be adjusted to suit our reactions: otherwise the total consumption and production of particular articles will not match. The reluctant purchaser must be tempted by price reductions, "bargain" sales and so forth; and the strong buyer's market must be held in check by upward movements of price, where demand is outrunning current supply. In cases where these conditions may be thought too harsh, points or rations must be substituted for, or used in addition to, full money. In other words, where the price of full consumer freedom is felt to be too high, this freedom will be given up, or at least restricted by the use of one of the intermediate methods already described in our discussion of points. Policy must turn upon the value set upon this particular freedom in relation to other social ends.

I cannot refrain from expressing the personal hope that that value will be high. Even in the case of the most fundamental necessities, it seems that individual consumption can only be standardized at the expense of quite serious disregard of personal preferences. One proof of this lies in the persistent private barter of rations which goes on at present in circumstances in which strict rationing is, after all, only applied to quite few of the articles which we consume, and those only the ones where it might be supposed that needs and habits would be reasonably uniform. Nevertheless, daily experience shows that there are the widest divergences of opinion between household and household as to where the shoe pinches most. No doubt the Ministry of Food has accurate data about all this; but every housewife knows how easy it is to find people willing and anxious to exchange sugar for magarine or lard for tea and vice versa, and how everybody's grumble is different from his neighbor's. Moreover, it does seem that many women at least (and half the population is female) find quite an important personal satisfaction in the exercise of consumer choice. The pleasure of shopping (when it was a pleasure) was not simply the pleasure of acquisition. It was a form, even if a humble form, of the satisfaction derived from the expression of personality; from the exercise of choice, taste, forethought and careful planning. Scope for the exercise of these faculties naturally increases as the level of income rises. The housewife with only a pound in her bag and a large and voracious family to feed cannot afford to consider more than a tiny selection from the million and more possible alternative ways in which that pound can be spent in any average shopping district. But, even at the lowest levels, there is some scope for choice—as the divergences of personal budgets in the same income-groups show. And in planning, as we reasonably may plan, for a rising standard of living, we should not dismiss a freedom as unimportant merely because it has comparatively little significance to the very poor. It is a rational hope that the very poor we shall not always have with us.

Rations, and semi-rations such as points, rank, therefore, I suggest, as definitely inferior methods of distribution, as a general rule, to distribution by sale for ordinary money that is available for the purchase of anything at any time. The words "as a general rule" are important, for one should not be dogmatic about this: there may be a case for tokens of restricted validity or limited life in particular instances. It is not, I think, certain, that family allowances, which are necessarily payable *to* an adult *for* a child, should take the form of money which can be spent on articles that no child needs or ought to have. In cases like this there is at least a case to argue. But a bias in favor of money as an instrument for distributing consumables is a bias in favor of freedom, and it is on that account a useful bias to start with. As our means become more ample, and the scale of personal consumption can be enlarged, so distribution by money may in time give way, not to tokens of a more rigid character, but to an extension of the range of goods supplied without stint or price at all. That, I think, is the hopeful line of advance. Unrestricted free distribution is the only method which gives actually greater freedom to the consumer than does straightforward sale for money. The time may come when it will seem as absurd to pay a fare on a bus, as it would to put a penny in a slot-meter every time you use your private lavatory. The question what goods and services should be added to the free list, and when, may prove one of the most interesting and controversial topics of the next few generations. In the meantime, until we can step forward towards these more lavish methods of distribution, it seems better to stay where we are (or were before the war) and stick to money, rather than to step backwards into methods that permit only a more limited freedom.

CHAPTER IV

The Freedom of the Consumer

II. CONSUMERS' SOVEREIGNTY

W E MUST now take up the more fundamental issues raised by the larger claims for consumers' sovereignty which can be read into the demand for freedom to spend our money "as we please." These necessarily involve a somewhat abstract discussion. Those who have not acquired a taste for this should proceed at once to Chapter V. They may do so with greater readiness, since, on page 68, they will find that the freedom described as consumers' sovereignty has one peculiar quality: namely, that nobody unversed in economic analysis, would know from ordinary experience whether this freedom was his or not—as he would know from ordinary experience whether he was, or was not, free to buy more than a fixed ration of cheese, or whether he was, or was not, free to leave his job. The incompatibility of economic planning with consumers' sovereignty is, however, one of the chief arguments used by those professional economists who are opponents of planning. The subject cannot, therefore, be ignored.

Consumer sovereignty implies, as we have seen, that the pattern of production should be determined by the actual choices that the consumer makes amongst the goods that are offered to him for sale—by the ballot-box of the market place, in fact. The underlying principle is sometimes loosely expressed in such terms as these: where the consumer is sovereign, the production of things that sell readily will be increased, while the output of those that find a poor market will be diminished. This, however, is not nearly precise enough. For the question of marketability is always bound up with the question of price. If, for instance, two types of radiogram are put on the market, one priced at twenty guineas and one at thirty, and the first sells briskly while the second attracts few buyers, the principle of consumer sovereignty does not necessarily demand that the output of the first should be expanded at the expense of the second. Before we can give that answer, we must know how the respective selling prices were arrived at. Suppose that the actual labor and materials required for manufacture in the two cases are the same; then the slow sale of the second is not due to the fact that people want it less than the first, but simply that for some reason or other they are being overcharged for it. No correct inferences about consumer demand can be made until both are offered at the same price. Obviously the attractiveness of an article that is offered for sale greatly depends upon its price, and can never be considered apart from this. It follows that unless selling prices are fixed in some way that is not just arbitrary, but is itself under the rule of consumer sovereignty, sales will be just as much influenced by the policy of whoever has power to fix prices as by the preferences of consumers.

Suppose, now, that the second radiogram is of a more elaborate character, costing fifty per cent more to produce but giving better reproduction. Accepting for the moment the (large and unverified) assumption that public buying is a safe guide to public wanting, then we are entitled to say that since the number of those who think the superior merits of the better set great enough to justify the extra cost involved has been overestimated, consumer sovereignty demands a larger output of the cheaper, and a smaller output of the more expensive model. We can, in fact, only draw conclusions about what pattern of production best pleases consumers, when we are sure that all the articles offered for sale are being produced in the most economical possible way, and offered at the most economical possible price.

Equally no such conclusions can be drawn unless we are sure that goods are not deliberately subsidized from other sources in order to make possible their sale at a price actually lower than their cost of production. For if the first radiogram is only sold at twenty guineas because there is a ten-guinea government subsidy on every set, then again the voice of the consumer is distorted. His apparent preference for this model is only due to the fact that it has been artificially cheapened. If he were asked to pay the full cost of both sets, the sales of the first would fall away, since some who would buy it for twenty guineas will not think it worth thirty. In effect, the principle of consumer sovereignty boils down (or up!) to this. If everything is put on sale at the most economical possible unsubsidized price, then everything that is sold at that price is judged by the sovereign consumer to have been worth making, and everything which is unsold is voted down by him, as not having been worth the labor and materials and other expenses necessarily incurred in its manufacture. Unsold goods, or goods which can only be sold by reduc-

ing their price below cost of production, are in fact judged
on this criterion to be waste, in exactly the same way as a
person will judge that he has wasted his time if he has
done a job (mended a shoe for instance) and subsequently expresses the opinion that it wasn't worth doing.
In this latter case the statement is tantamount to a declara-
tion that the speaker would have been more advantageously employed doing something other than shoe mend-
ing. In the former case, the consumer's judgment is that
the labor and materials used in making articles that cannot be sold for their full cost of production would have
been more advantageously devoted to making something
else.

It is important to notice that this kind of judgment applies to every individual article or unit of service of every
kind. In the example of the radiograms just given, if both
are priced at their minimum cost, and demand for one
outstrips supply, while in the other case supplies exceed
the demand for them, the consumer's judgment does not
imply that the second model ought not to have been produced at all. It is a judgment that production ought to be
switched from the second to the first model just up to and
not beyond the point at which both will be selling
smoothly (always of course at the minimum unsubsidized
price), with demand and supply just keeping pace. If the
thirty-guinea set is really a superior model, it will find
some buyers who judge it worth the extra money. All that
went wrong was that the number of such buyers was overestimated. It follows that if the pattern of production
faithfully adapts itself to the directions of the consumer
it has at least a precise quantitative instruction to follow.
The adaption takes place, to be sure, through a continu-

ous process of trial and error, demand being overestimated here, and underestimated there; but at least the quality and quantity of the errors are objectively demonstrated.

This detailed quantitative judgment applies moreover not only to such matters as the appropriate scale of production of one radio model relatively to another, but also to the relative claims on the productive resources of the country of goods which have no such intimate relation with one another. For the determination of economic priorities necessarily involves such vast decisions as settling the quantity of labor and materials to be allocated to the manufacture of cosmetics (and within that total the amount to be assigned to each particular variety of each particular species of cosmetic) as against the quantity of labor and materials to be devoted to the production of foodstuffs (and within that total the amount to be assigned to each particular variety of each particular species of food). Some materials are, of course, specific in the sense that they cannot be used for all purposes: in such cases the scope of choice is, perhaps mercifully, restricted. But others, like coal, are necessary in a vast variety of different processes. Happily in a going community these staggeringly complex decisions never have to be made, so to speak, from scratch. They always take the form of adding something here, and subtracting something there, to and from existing totals. In the switch from peace to war, and the switch from war to peace production, these additions and subtractions become very large sums indeed, and the previous pattern of production in consequence undergoes remarkable changes. In the less frantic days of peace, the movements, whatever the machinery by which they are made, are on a smaller scale. At all times, however, and in all circumstances, the pattern of production ultimately comes down to a matter of minutest detail. It is not only a question of broad decisions, say, about the priority claims of houses and schools on the resources of the building industry. It is a question of whether this particular house or school is, or is not, to be built in this particular way in this particular place at this particular time. And ultimately, by one method or another, that question is in fact always settled.

I emphasize the detail and complexity, and the range of possible variety, of the pattern of production, because the strongest argument in favor of settling economic priorities on the principle of consumer sovereignty is the argument that the actual purchases of consumers provide the only record which can indicate what the people really want in terms sufficiently precise and detailed to enable the pattern of production to conform to those wants. This is indeed the strongest argument in the armory of the wholehearted anti-planners. Polls of public opinion, schemes of market research and so forth, may give at most detailed indications of a few people's preferences in a limited part of the field, or an outline of the broad choices of larger numbers over the whole. But no ballot, other than the ballot of the market place, it is said, can both cover the whole field and give the necessary detail. If, therefore, the consumer is to have what he really wants, production must follow the market. The consumer, and not the planner acting by the light of nature, or by such crude tests as he can devise as substitutes for the automatic records of actual sales, must be sovereign.

This is a grand theory. But, unhappily, it is impossible to express this theory in any manageable compass with-

out serious ambiguity in some of its most critical terms.
Books have been written to clear up these ambiguities;
but since I cannot make an excursus here on the scale of
these books, I have simply had to leave the terms open to
the best construction that anybody can put upon them.
But for practical purposes these ambiguities are serious.
For instance, the whole of the argument as summarized
above turns on the phrase "minimum possible economic
price" or minimum necessary cost of production. Market
purchases only accurately register the scale of consumers'
demand if goods are priced exactly at this level. How is
this figure to be defined in theory or determined in practice? A great part of economic literature is occupied with
its definition and analysis. What elements should it include
or exclude? To what extent can it be accurately reflected
in the actual costing figures of actual firms? In all this
discussion it is perhaps safe to say that there is substantial
agreement on two points. First, this minimal cost of production can only be competitively determined. The only
hope of reaching it is to leave the door always open in
every industry and trade for everyone to try and do better (that is to say, to produce more economically) than
everyone else. The minimum economical price of a given
output of, say, radiograms of a given type may thus be
said to be the lowest price at which that output can be
put on the market in conditions in which there is unrestricted or perfect competition between all the firms in the
industry and between the workers working for them (and,
it may be added, also between all the firms supplying the
materials needed for the manufacture of these radiograms
and all the workers working for *them* also). Even that
elaborate sentence conceals a multitude of complexities,

for "perfect competition" is certainly not self-explanatory. These difficulties must, however, be passed by for the time being. The second point about the definition of minimum economical price on which there seems to be general agreement is that some elements in this cost inevitably fail to get included in market prices, even under the most cunning systems of cost calculation. These are the elements which do not directly affect anybody actually engaged in the production of the goods whose price we are considering, but nevertheless fall inescapably on some other party who is not in a position to charge the actual producer for any loss that he may suffer. An example often quoted is the damage and defacement to buildings generally caused by the presence of smoky factories in their neighborhood. The goods that come out of these factories are not charged with the cost of the destruction for which their manufacture is thus indirectly responsible. If they were, this would make them slightly more expensive and the consumer's judgment as to the proper scale of their production would need to be revised in the light of this new, higher, price. Ingenious minds can find a very great number of cases in which what may be called the social cost of production exceeds the direct money cost to the producer in this kind of way. Market prices, which are all the data that the consumer knows, are thus distorted from the beginning.

All this means that the practical prospects of the consumer exercising full sovereignty in this sense fall far short of the theoretical case which can be made out for his reign. To sum up: in the first place we do not know precisely what the minimum economical price of any article means. We think that it is synonymous with the competitive price, or the price that would be reached in a state of perfect competition. We do not know, except perhaps in an extremely abstract sense, what a regime of perfect competition implies. We fear that even under that regime certain essential data, relevant for effective consumer judgment, would be unavoidably lacking.

And to crown all, we have no reason to suppose that anything approaching this regime of perfect competition exists, or ever has existed or is likely to exist. On the contrary, all the evidence shows that we are traveling rapidly away from it. This need not of course be a final argument, if the direction of travel could be easily reversed, or at least if the possible advantages of reversing it would offer attractions great enough to justify facing any obstacles in the way. Actually, however, these conditions can hardly be said to obtain. It is conceivable that, if we had taken a different turning in the nineteenth century, it might have been possible deliberately to foster a very much wider and more open competition than even then existed; though American experiments in trust-busting are not very encouraging here. But, for technical reasons, the shape which modern industry has taken is ill-adapted to a world of genuinely open and free and universal competition. In many industries the amount of plant and other capital necessary to start business at all is so enormous that all the scales are weighted against the newcomer and in favor of the already well-established firm. In other cases, competition in itself involves waste, as is recognized in local public utilities like the supply of gas and water and local transport. And on top of these technical conditions we have the persistent and, we must add, officially sponsored, trend away from competition towards deliberate organization of markets. If we cast our minds back only as far as the England of the nineteen-thirties we step into a world with organized restraint of competition in coal, shipping, shipbuilding, cotton, steel, and a great many agricultural products, not to mention get-togethers of local tradesmen throughout the country, or the domination of giants like I.C.I. or Unilever, or the total disregard of freedom in international trade, or the control of the labor market by Trade Unions and employers' associations. These are, moreover, just a few of the more conspicuous examples which leap to the mind, and not, of course, anything in the way of an exhaustive list. If effective consumer sovereignty depends on freedom of competition, there is a mighty heap of eggs to be unscrambled.

And there still remain further, and fundamental, criticisms on the doctrine that even if these practical difficulties could be overcome, consumer sovereignty would, in fact, result in a more efficient machinery for registering what people want than anything else that can be invented. First, we have the old, familiar (and solid) criticism that unjustifiable plural voting is permitted in the ballot-box of the market place. The fact that I am willing to pay five shillings for what you will only buy at half-a-crown is not necessarily proof that my want is twice as great as yours, or that it should (as under a rule of consumer sovereignty it would) count for twice as much in determining the pattern of production. The difference in the intensity of our respective money demands may merely be due to a difference in the amount of money which we have at our disposal. Willingness to pay for an article is always compounded of two elements, namely, a desire to have the article and a willingness to part with the necessary money. Of course the second element is affected by a person's whole financial position, and will vary according as he feels himself to be in funds or not. Hence the first premise of the theory of consumer sovereignty is frequently laughed out of court by critics who point out, quite reasonably, that substantial differences between the incomes of different classes makes the money demand for an article an entirely misleading index of the intensity with which it is desired. The orthodox answer to this question seems to be that, if you cannot infer the urgency of a person's need for an article objectively from the amount of money which he is willing to pay for it, you cannot compare the urgencies of different people's needs in any scientific and accurate way at all. This is rather like defending a faulty pair of scales by saying that, if you do not weigh out your stuff on these, you cannot measure its weight at all. If it is true that no other scales are available, the only sensible answer is that accurate measurement is in the circumstances impossible. One must rely on general judgments, or frank guess work. The fact that correct scales are not to be had does not make incorrect ones right. The analogy holds, I suggest, completely. We may admit at once that no other method of registering what people *want* can compare in detail and accuracy with the record which market purchases provide of what people *will buy*. If, however, what people will buy and what they want are two different things, not related in any precisely determinate mathematical way, then the beautiful delicacy of this instrument for recording what people will buy, in no way commends its use to those who are interested only in discovering what it is that they want.

All this means that, if the phrase "freedom to spend our money as we like" means freedom, by so spending it, to get out of the economic system whatever we most want, it is, in any precise sense, a Utopian freedom; and it is not, of course, a pleasure that we have ever anywhere enjoyed. It is true that, in a world where private enterprise generally prevails, goods are not made unless their manufacture is thought sufficiently profitable by those who make them. But the meaning of "sufficiently profitable" in a matter of opinion. When sellers and manufacturers are able to get together and agree upon a common interpretation of this expression, "a sufficiently profitable price" usually turns out to mean something comfortably above our "minimum competitive value." In consequence commodities which many consumers would have estimated as worth the cost of their competitive manufacture but no more, may never see the light at all. In the world of the greatest consumer liberty that we have ever known, the pattern of production was never quantitatively and qualitatively shaped to suit even the relative money demands of consumers, much less their wishes. The weakness of the thorough-going critics of conscious determination of economic priorities is that they constantly compare an ideal, theoretical consumer sovereignty (in which demand corresponds precisely to desire and all production is competitive) with the actualities of planning in a world of flesh and blood and imperfect human institution.[1]

1. This defect seems to me to underly the whole thesis of books like Professor Hayek's *Road to Serfdom*. One would be in a better position to assess the value of his diatribes against the planners if he showed any appreciation of the evils which have given rise, at least on the part of public-spirited persons, to a demand for planning. The alternatives are not planning or Utopia; they are plan-

If the rule of the consumer in the market will not give us the demonstrably ideal pattern of production, nothing else will. If the scales turn out to be faulty, we can only fall back on the much more crude and clumsy apparatus of general judgments—those judgments that are made "by the representatives of all on behalf of all." [2] It is, therefore, at this point that we reach the conclusion, forecast in Chapter I, that the problem of determining the best possible use for the resources of any community is scientifically insoluble. But at this point also we take comfort from the analogy there suggested with the choice of a partner in marriage. Just as everybody knows the difference between a happily and an unhappily married couple (especially the couple themselves) so, with commonsense, good judgment, and good social institutions, we shall know the difference between a community which is reasonably contented with its economic arrangements and one which is not.

There is the less reason to be depressed about the Utopian nature of full consumer sovereignty, because, after all, it is questionable whether this is a freedom which people really value highly. Liberty of consumption in the narrow sense—that is, liberty to choose as your taste and pocket dictate from the stuff you find upon the market—

---

ning, for better or for worse, and a planless world to which very serious exception can be taken on good grounds. Professor Hayek is inclined (see, for example, pp. 17 ff. of *The Road to Serfdom*) to argue that the defects of a system in which economic priorities are not consciously determined are not inherent, and could be overcome by resort to measures which are well within our grasp. It is greatly to be hoped that he will write another book elaborating this constructive aspect of his thesis. Otherwise it seems that the only choice is frying pan or fire.

2. See above, p. 19.

certainly does rank high, as we have seen. But liberty of consumption in the more far-reaching sense of power to determine through consumption the quantitative pattern of production is a different matter. Liberty of consumption in this sense is a highly sophisticated concept. It can hardly be said that people greatly prize a freedom the nature of which they do not fully understand, and the presence or absence of which they would not even recognize!

These last few words are important. The real reason why full consumer sovereignty is not a matter that people trouble about is that they are generally unaware whether they have got that freedom or not. By and large, the pattern of production is a matter which the individual has to take as a datum under any system, planned or not. In the Soviet Union the appearance of bicycles in the shops is the result, and is known to be the result, of the conscious decision of the planning authorities to give a priority to the manufacture of bicycles. In this country it would be a mark, and would be known to be a mark, of some manufacturer's anticipation of profit. But for the vast majority of us either the bicycles are there or they are not there, either they are priced at a figure which we are prepared to pay or they are beyond our reach, and that is the end of it. If, by some beautiful miracle, full consumer sovereignty on the textbook model could be established, it is a curious fact that everything would look just the same to the individual consumer. Once more the bicycles would either be there, or they would not be there, they would either be priced at a figure which a particular consumer was prepared to pay, or they would not be so priced. Let us say that the price is £5. Consumer sovereignty or not, any consumer who refrained from paying that price would be registering a decision that he could not spare £5 for a bicycle. This he would know. But, in the special case of consumer sovereignty, he would also be casting one vote for the opinion that the labor and materials used in making that bicycle could have been better employed in making something else. This he would not know. It is more likely that he would in all cases grumble at the high price of the bicycle. If he had been brought up in good socialist doctrine, he might (for all the efficiency of consumer sovereignty in "giving the public just what the public wants") also be heard to murmur that bicycles should be made for use and not for profit.

CHAPTER V

The Freedom of the Consumer

III. FREEDOM TO SAVE

So MUCH for the subtleties of freedom to spend our money *as* we like. There remains the final clause— "and when we like." Freedom to distribute expenditure through time means, of course, both freedom to spend at a particular time, and freedom to refrain from spending. To avoid confusions of terminology (which proliferate in this field) we will say that anybody who has money in his pocket or in the bank, but is not at the moment spending that money, is saving. Very probably if a person accumulates a considerable sum by such saving, his intention is subsequently, as he would say, to invest it. He means, in fact, to buy out of his savings something from which he hopes to derive further income (like railway stock or National Savings Bonds); or something from which he hopes to get lasting use (like a house to live in); or he intends himself to go into business with his savings (as by renting a factory and hiring workers to make typewriters there). All these are alternative uses for saved money. When saved money is eventually disposed of in any of these ways it will, on our terminology, be said to be no longer "saved" (in spite of the fact that in another context it would be absurd to say that a man's savings are

70

no longer saved when he has built a house with them).
We may even say that to make an investment with saved
money is in effect to spend that money (in spite of con-
trasts, which are proper and useful in other contexts, between spending and investing). Freedom to distribute
money through time is then equivalent to freedom to
choose between saving and not-saving, or between saving
and one or other form of spending. It is, in fact, the freedom to spend "when you like."

This is a freedom which the public certainly under-
stands. It is difficult to say how high it ranks in the scale
of values, but it undoubtedly has a place. People want to
"save up for" all sorts of things. Even in Soviet Russia,
where there is virtually no scope for investment in private
business, there are weddings and funerals and great occasions, when it is good to have more than a week's wages
in hand; and it is as patriotic there as it is here to subscribe as much as possible to government loans. We may
fairly say that the ordinary person, in any kind of society
where money is used, sets store by being able to plan the
spending of this money as he chooses, at least during his
own life time.

Now this almost certainly means that an average individual will spend some part of his income *irregularly*
through time. The more margin he has over day-to-day
necessities, the more likely is this to be true; but in a
small way it will be true even of the very poorest. People
with small incomes, and to a less extent others also, will
indeed attempt to regularize their spending through membership of clothing clubs, or by taking out insurances to
meet sudden demands for expenditure for which they
fear that they will not have ready money in hand. To get

a complete picture of what money is spent and what is saved, we ought to take account of the use which is made of these club subscriptions and insurance premiums by the clubs and insurance companies to whom they are for the time being intrusted. If, however, we remember that these organizations also either spend or save their incomes, and that that is true of everybody who has any money anywhere at any moment, we need not complicate the picture further. We can make a general presumption that any individual's spending is likely, if he is free to do what he chooses, to be irregularly distributed through time.

This means that unless the irregularities of different people's spending dovetail neatly into one another, the total outlay of the public as a whole will be irregularly distributed through time. In an unstable and changing world it seems that that kind of neat dovetailing could only happen as the result of a most remarkable coincidence. It would be the more remarkable in any world where there was considerable scope for private investment, as there was in this country before the war; for investors are very nervous and touchy people (as witness the history of speculative booms and slumps), and they suffer also from time to time from unaccountable fits of both optimism and pessimism. When some people think that business is good, there is a marked tendency for other people to think that business is good, and vice versa; so that there is also a marked tendency for money which has been saved up by many different people, with the intention of making an investment, all to come out of its hiding at the same time. Similarly when the wait-and-see mentality gets around, people have a way of all prolonging their savings together, and all holding off from spending what they have accumulated in some investment or business venture. It is, therefore, a reasonable assumption that, if everybody has freedom to time his own spending, and to save as much and as long as he chooses, the total spending of everybody taken together will proceed in a series of fits and starts.

There we come into conflict with another objective which is almost universally acclaimed now as essential in any civilized society: that is full employment. The simple doctrine that everybody's job depends on somebody else's spending or investing was known to the man in the street long before it was proclaimed by the economists. Every time anybody puts by a few shillings for a rainy day he is to that extent withholding the means of somebody else's employment. Obviously, if nobody spent anything, nobody else would have any work. Obviously, also, if spending is intermittent, employment will be intermittent; and, if the total amount spent, year in year out, by all the community taken together is not sufficient to provide employment for everybody in the labor market, there will be a standing margin of unemployment. It follows that there is here a possible, and serious, conflict of liberties. So long as a man's or woman's income is normally dependent on his or her ability to find paid employment, an unemployed person is an income-less person. And an income-less person is a person who is free only to set about getting himself an income. The liberty of the consumer to distribute his spending as he likes through time is thus a potential threat to the liberty of the worker to do more than look for work.

The fact has thus to be faced that full employment is

impossible, if the timing of *all* outlay is determined by the personal whims of individual consumers. This is one of the occasions when we are at war with ourselves. The liberty of the consumer-self threatens the security of the producer-self; for *the same person* wants both to spend and save as he pleases, and always to be sure of a job. Not enough weight is given to this conflict by the advocates of complete freedom of consumers' choice: it is for instance never so much as mentioned in Professor Hayek's *Road to Serfdom*. For full employment is incompatible, not only with the theoretical ideal of consumers' sovereignty as defined in the preceding chapter: it is incompatible equally with the bastard sovereignty of the consumer which does duty for this idea in practice—with any system, in fact, in which production is left to follow the dictates of market purchases. Under any such system not only must the quality and character of production faithfully follow the quality and character of consumer-spending; the total volume of production of all kinds must also shrink and swell as the public happens to tighten or relax its purse strings. And, to judge from experience, even when those strings are at their slackest, and spending is most generous, the total reached will rarely, if ever, be great enough to provide work for all who want and need it. Even in the best years there has usually been far too large a margin of employable unemployed.[1] Full employment does not happen of itself.

Happily there is every reason to hope that this conflict between consumer liberty and producer security can be

1. In the years from 1921 to 1939 inclusive, the annual average percentage of workers unemployed in Great Britain never fell below 9.6 per cent.

resolved: and resolved without grave interference with the consumer's liberty to spend as he pleases. But it cannot be resolved without a considerable amount of economic planning. The road out of the difficulty lies not through dictating to the consumer when he may or may not spend his money; but through the state's undertaking both to make good the deficiencies, and to compensate for the vagaries, of consumer spending. The task of adjusting, one way or another, the total amount of spending by public authorities and private persons to the total capacity and demands of the labor market must become a public responsibility. This means that the state must do a new kind of sum. It must add up the total amount of spending (which, we must remember, in this context includes what is generally called investing) necessary to find work for all, estimate the total volume of spending by private and business consumers, and be prepared itself at the least to fill the gap by the purchases of government departments and other public authorities. These purchases will, of course, affect the pattern of production and, as far as they go, amount to a conscious determination of economic priorities. Thus, if the spending of public authorities takes the form of a large building program, unemployed workers (together with some who may be drawn from other employments) will be busy with the manufacture of bricks and mortar (or, alternatively, of prefabricated units). The new houses which result will have come into existence not as the result of the unconscious working of the market, but through the deliberate decision of responsible people. And that is planning.

The theory which underlies this policy of the maintenance of employment by planned public spending is now generally accepted. It is for instance implicit in the government's White Paper on Employment Policy,[2] though the practical applications suggested there are decidedly timid. For our purpose it is necessary only to emphasize that there are *two* variables in our sum:—the total of private consumer outlay and the total outlay of public authorities must *together* add up to the amount necessary for full employment. The question, which of these components—consumer or state spending—should take priority, is a question of policy which different communities can decide in different ways according to their several scales of social value. Either component can be taken as a datum and the other adjusted to match. In no country is the need to maintain full employment the sole criterion of when, where, and how much public authorities should spend. Expenditure on the education of children, for instance, is not undertaken simply for the purpose of finding employment for teachers. In the Soviet Union before the war, first priority, particularly in the earlier plans, was given to public outlay on new construction; such resources as were left after provision for the construction program were then available to meet the needs of consumers. In all countries in time of war, first priority goes to government purchase of war materials. In this country, in the absence of any fundamental change of social outlook, it seems likely that the attitude of government towards private spending after the war will be somewhat deferential. The White Paper plainly thinks of a state employment program as supplementing, rather than supplanting, the outlay of private persons and private business.

Experiment will show the conditions for the success-

2. *Employment Policy*. Cmd. 6527 of 1944.

ful pursuit of such a policy and the possible variations
which can be played upon the main theme. After two
wars, we do at least *know* that full employment is possible, provided only that the state is prepared, directly
or indirectly, to become an employer on a sufficiently
large scale. We do not yet know how far full employment
can be attained by a delicate balance between employment on government and on private work, or where that
balance must be struck. From the angle of consumer-
liberty, however, one cheerful forecast can reasonably be
made. Of all the different forms of spending, it is, as we
have already said, spending for investment which is the
most irregular and the most unreliable. The total of what
people spend on food and clothes and household goods
and holidays and drink and smokes—even on weddings and
funerals—is in the aggregate much less liable to unpre-
dictable upheavals—except for one simple and familiar
reason. What makes this total go up and down is not our
inconstant spending of a given income, so much as fluc-
tuation in the amount of income that we have. But the
amount of spendable income that we have itself depends
primarily—for the great majority—on work and wages:
and work and wages are determined in their turn by the
general state of the business world, on the one hand—that
is, by the willingness of investors to launch out into new
business—and, on the other hand, by the scale of employment offered by the demands of public authorities.

It follows that variations in spending for enjoyment are
consequential results, more than primary causes, of unemployment. Of course it is a vicious circle: the greatest
cause of unemployment is unemployment. But the unemployed are not the cause of unemployment because of

their passion for intermittent saving and irregular spending. They create unemployment by their lack of the wherewithal either to spend or to save. It follows that the timing of the ordinary expenditure of ordinary people is not the critical factor in the causation of unemployment: the critical factor is the timing of investment. Security of employment need not, therefore, and should not, demand interference with the private person's right to distribute his personal expenditure on goods and services for his own immediate consumption through time according to his fancy. How far it will necessitate control of the distribution through time of private *investment* expenditure will depend upon how far the state finds it necessary to adopt an independent role in the planning of production. If the public authorities seek to confine themselves in their employment policy to attempts to counterbalance the ups and downs of private investment, they will be following, not making, a pattern, and such control will be kept to a minimum. This appears to be present Government policy.[3]

Sir William Beveridge, in his *Full Employment in a Free Society*,[4] has forcefully argued that more than this will be necessary if we are to achieve full employment, and not merely to stabilize unemployment at a level half-way between the bad and the not very good years of the past. If, however, such a more active policy is pursued, private persons and concerns cannot retain the freedom to make substantial investments exactly as and when they choose. For public authorities and private purchasers cannot (both) buy the same things at the same time; nor can they even try to do so without disastrous consequences.

3. See the White Paper on *Employment Policy*, 1944.
4. London: George Allen & Unwin, Ltd.

CHAPTER VI

The Freedom of the Producer

I. CHOICE OF EMPLOYMENT

I

IT IS stupid and inefficient to make a plan and then to fail to carry it out. It follows that, in so far as the production of particular goods and services is deliberately planned, people, plant, and materials must somehow be got together on the job of producing those goods and services. The problem here is just how to get those people, plant, and materials together on definite jobs, without violating the liberty of the people.

So long as most of us work for wages, interest will naturally center on such issues as freedom to choose our work, and freedom to fix, or to have some say in fixing, our wages. In the discussion of these liberties, however, a new point arises which had no relevance to the liberty of the consumer. Producer freedoms can be restricted in two alternative ways: by force of law, or by force of economic pressure. Thus, effective freedom to choose your work implies both that you cannot be sent to prison or fined for refusing to take a particular job, and that you are not in such desperate financial straits that you must accept the first offer that comes. The sanction is thus either legal or economic. In the case of consumer liberties, on the other hand, a legal sanction is hardly ever practicable. The consumer who is deprived of all choice of consumption has only the alternatives of taking his rations or leaving them. It is seldom practicable (and would even more seldom be necessary) to punish people by law for their failure to consume goods which the authorities have provided for their use. Parents are indeed, from time to time, fined for failure to send their children to school, and men have been imprisoned for refusing to wear military uniform; but these are plainly exceptional cases.

In our discussion of the impact of planning upon the freedoms that particularly interest the employed worker, we shall deal first with the possibility of limitation by legal sanctions, and afterwards with the use of economic, or apparently economic, compulsion.[1] Critical members of our society sometimes impatiently dismiss the whole question of legal sanctions as unimportant, on the ground that the economic limitations upon the worker's freedom are so powerful, that any legal regulations are mere trivialities. I do not think that this attitude is justified, and particularly I do not think that it is borne out by the experience of legal restrictions (which are now alterna-

1. Throughout this and the following chapter, I shall assume that economic planning has been successfully directed at least to the maintenance of full employment (in the sense that the number of available vacancies normally exceeds the number of persons looking for work) on the lines suggested in the preceding chapter. This seems a proper assumption to make, first, because the public demands and expects that unemployment shall not be allowed to return after the war, and the Government has taken responsibility for trying to fulfill this expectation; and second, because the assumption of full employment aggravates the problems of choice of employment and freedom of collective bargaining, and therefore compels us to face any difficulties in the most acute form in which they are likely to arise.

tives, not additions, to economic compulsions) during the war. But even if such criticism were justified in, say, the England of the nineteen-thirties, we should still have to consider what are the risks and what would be the consequences of legal restriction on producer freedoms, in circumstances in which economic pressure is relaxed or removed.

There are several reasons for treating legal restrictions as in a class apart—possibly as grade for grade more serious than economic compulsions. A fine of 20s. is certainly less of a catastrophe than six months' fruitless search for a job and an income. But the comparatively serious character of legal limitations of liberty at every level, springs largely from the fact that, as things are, conviction for a breach of the law carries certain social consequences, which do not attach in the same way to economic misfortunes. Economic misfortunes can, at least, up to a point, be ascribed to the will of God, or to an economic system whose ways are accepted as inscrutable. But a legal conviction is demonstrably the result of a breach of man-made law. And for that an offender incurs the opprobrium associated with wrong-doing. Perhaps legal conviction *ought* not to carry these consequences; but, in fact, it does, and so long as that is true there is a qualitative difference between a legal and an economic sanction. As long as a man who finds his job intolerable is entitled to ask for his cards and leave, he can weigh up the financial risks, and, if he thinks these worth facing, he can discharge himself without, as the saying is, a stain on his reputation. But if he is legally bound to his job, his reputation will be deeply involved, should he decide to defy the law and walk out. He can never again appear in court with "no previous

convictions." It is true that, with the modern multiplication of possible occasions of offense, many people now get
into the courts on one account or another, who would
have been horrified to find themselves there a few years
back; and the public may, in consequence, cease to take
a very serious view of convictions for breach of the rules
and regulations incidental to economic planning or for
similar offenses. But is it a good defense of an extended
use of legal sanctions to plead that law-breaking is no
longer held to be a matter of morals?

Further, the fact that legal regulations are universally
recognized as man-made seems to provoke much more
general resentment against any curtailment of liberty involved than is felt when the compulsion is economic.
There are exceptions to this rule, but the man who remarked: "I do not feel frustrated if I am prevented from
making a voyage to the West Indies because I have not
enough money to pay the fare, but I do resent some
official telling me that I am not to go," seems to be voicing
an opinion which is widely shared. The exceptions are
found amongst those who realize that economic frustrations are also the result of institutions which are man-
made and therefore changeable; but this requires a
considerable, and relatively rare, degree of sophistication.
This tendency to distinguish between what may be called
personal and impersonal restrictions, and to accept the
latter with comparative equanimity, is, I think, carried
too far in contemporary England. But if we are to take
account of what people feel about freedom, it certainly
has to be brought into the picture as a real psychological
fact, and as additional ground for regarding legal prohibi-

tions as likely to cause frustrations more grievous than those due to economic necessity.

For the age-groups liable to military service or industrial direction, the urgencies of war have completely suspended legal freedom of choice of employment. In a life-or-death situation, hardly anyone challenges the necessity of these measures. But war experience has given us a good enough taste of life without this freedom for us to form some estimate of how much we prize it. Perhaps, some day, Mass Observation will give us one of their vivid human pictures of the great toll of daily frustration and unhappiness exacted from men and women now bound to uncongenial jobs. Certainly common observation tells enough of the story for the time being. Choice of employment is a fundamental liberty.

Actually this particular freedom is two-sided. It involves, first, a man's freedom to choose the *kind* of work that he will do, and, second, his right to accept or refuse a *particular* job. The second, which is in a sense the narrower liberty, is probably the one about which most people feel most keenly: partly, perhaps, because most of us, certainly after we are well-established in adult life, have not enough imagination to see ourselves following some quite different occupation, and to yearn after this. It takes no imagination, however, to feel the daily irritations of the distasteful job—the uncongenial companions, the inconvenient hours, the long journey, the unjust and petty foreman. Nor should we under-estimate the frustration of those who feel that they have drifted into the wrong line altogether, and especially of those who know themselves to have abilities beyond their present employments. The miner who longed for city life, the clerk who wanted to be a veterinary surgeon, the would-be teacher who drove a tram—these are just a handful of actual examples drawn from one person's acquaintances. A free society has to keep an eye on free choice both of vocation and of job.

A further distinction must, however, be made here. Freedom to *refuse* or to *leave* a job is not quite the same as freedom to *select* either one's job or one's vocation. Happily, there is nothing in the conscious determination of economic priorities which is inconsistent with the first of these freedoms—nothing which threatens the right to refuse or to leave a job, or which demands industrial conscription or compulsory direction. Whenever some industries are expanding and others contracting, there must, in all circumstances, be changes in the occupations of the people: but whether this expansion and contraction is accidental or planned need itself have no effect upon the machinery used to bring those changes about. In the sixteen years between 1923 and 1939, three-quarters of a million *additional* workers found their way into distributive occupations, more than 300,000 into building, and 60,000 into electrical engineering. Conversely, the number of workers classified as coal miners fell by nearly 400,000, the number of shipbuilders by nearly 95,000, and the number of cotton operatives by about 190,000. These changes, which were necessitated by unplanned and unforeseen variations in the prosperity of different industries, came about through the response of individuals to the opportunities, or lack of opportunities, open to them. People gravitate towards, and still more do they encourage their children to gravitate towards, the industries where pay and prospects look most promising. If pay and prospects and other conditions of employment are suitably adjusted, they will respond in just the same way to calls for fresh workers here or for reductions in staff there, when these changing demands reflect, not casual ups and downs of prosperity, but deliberate public policy. The workers necessary to carry through a large public program of housing, electrification, food production, or whatever it may be, can be engaged and employed in the ordinary commercial way. If the conditions of employment are sufficiently attractive (and training is provided where there is a shortage of necessary skills) the necessary labor will be forthcoming.

The parallel here with freedom of consumption is strictly accurate. The way to give free choice of consumption is to price the available goods and leave each consumer free to buy, or not to buy, as he pleases. The way to give free choice of employment is to price the jobs available and leave each worker free to apply for what he prefers. As with consumption, so also with employment, this is the method of inducement. Under this method, if the demand for certain very popular goods threatens to outrun supplies, the price must be raised in order to restrict buying. Under this method, if the demand for certain kinds of labor outruns the supply forthcoming, the price, that is, the wage, must be raised to attract further applicants. In both cases, of course, it is possible to use dictatorial methods instead of the method of inducement. A dictatorial government may prefer the former alternative; but that will be because it is dictatorial, not because it is engaged in economic planning.

It is indeed doubtful whether the method of compulsion in the distribution of workers between occupations and jobs can even plausibly be passed off as less trouble than the method of inducement. The producer freedoms stand, perhaps, here on firmer ground than the liberties of the consumer. The reason is that the direction of people to jobs is a much more complicated affair than the direction of—at any rate a large range of—goods to people. It is so much more difficult to find a satisfactory basis from which to start. To distribute, say, margarine on the basis of half a pound a head per week as the normal ration, with variations upwards or downwards for special classes, is a simple enough business. But you cannot run industry by allocating everybody, correspondingly, to a day's work a week in the mines. Industrial direction means getting down to the selection of the particular individuals destined for particular jobs—a colossal task in any large-scale program of production. Perhaps this is why the Soviet authorities, until war was practically at their frontiers, generally allowed free choice of vocation and employment, and made little use of industrial conscription, except in the case of political prisoners. Their wage and salary scales were deliberately framed so as to pay more for skills which were scarce, and less for those of which there was abundance; and the comrades seem to have responded with appropriate acquisitive alacrity.

From the angle of freedom, it is of course the great strength of selection by inducement that the actual individuals who get on to any particular job select themselves. The task of the planners is simply to estimate what rate of pay and other conditions of employment will attract the number of competent people required by the job in hand. This can be done only by a process of trial and error. It is also done by trial and error where there is no plan.

War experience, which is sometimes quoted as proof that extensive economic planning cannot be carried through without compulsory direction of labor, is quite misleading. Soviet experience to the contrary is much more convincing! For the first characteristic of war is hurry. In war there is no time to change the pattern of production by the less drastic, but necessarily more leisurely, methods of peace. While people were making up their minds what jobs they felt inclined to take, the war might have been lost: in consequence, everybody has to be ordered, or more politely, directed, on a very rough and ready basis of selection, into a job, and told to stay there till he is wanted somewhere else. Moreover, the violent changes in the pattern of production which war compels necessitate correspondingly violent changes, both upwards and downwards, in the demand for particular kinds of labor. Vast numbers of workers are wanted to make every part of airplanes, while the numbers retained on the production of gramophones is (apparently) reduced to nil. No doubt, if the wages in the airplane factories were fixed high enough, and those of the gramophone workers cut *sufficiently* drastically, the appropriate shift from the one industry to the other would take place. It would only come about, however, as the result of another upheaval—a violent redistribution of income between different sections of the employed population. Public feeling is, however, greatly outraged both by any heavy losses and by any spectacular gains which are directly caused by the impact of the war on our economy. Some such losses and gains have been tolerated, under protest.

But if we had relied on the market mechanism to effect the redistribution of labor necessitated by the war, they would have been nearly universal, and would certainly have been felt to be intolerable.

The third peculiarity of war is that what people want to do ceases to count. Freedom is in such danger that, paradoxically, it no longer matters. In war we have, as has been said, an exception to the rule that the particular form of organization known as the state should have no purposes beyond giving maximum scope to the several ends freely chosen by the citizens of whom it is composed. For the duration of the war, those citizens have, or are presumed to have, a common purpose which takes priority over all their several personal ends. The ground for this presumption is that unless the war is won, these individual purposes cannot be fulfilled, since the individuals who choose them will be either dead or enslaved.

None of this applies, or should apply, to a liberal economy in time of peace. What need is there then to be in such a hurry? Certainly we should not rank haste above freedom. Again, in peacetime, public opinion is less intolerant of changes in the economic position of different skills and occupational groups, partly because these changes are themselves less violent, and still more because the gains cannot be represented as the exploitation of a national calamity. And most important of all, in a free society, people's wishes do matter. In time of peace, if the only way to fill certain jobs is to force people into them under threat of fine or imprisonment, it is generally better that these jobs should be left undone. In saying this, we should not, of course, forget that it is impossible to know whether such drastic methods are the only way of getting things done, unless milder alternatives have been tried and have failed. There are, for example, serious penalties for failure to fulfill jury service in this country; but it does not follow that juries could not be recruited by any other means.

It is doubtful, however, whether legal freedom to *take* whatever job one pleases, or to choose one's occupation, should, or could be as absolute as freedom to *refuse* or *leave* a job. For the "method of inducement" works much more harshly in getting people out of places where they are not wanted, than it does in getting them into places where they are wanted. If, for instance, there is a 10 per cent surplus of labor in some industry, that method demands a relative reduction in the wages, not only of the surplus 10 per cent, but of all the workers employed in the industry. In a prosperous and expanding economy we might, to be sure, hope that "relative reduction" will generally mean nothing worse than staying put where you are, while others rise. Even so, since 90 per cent of the workers in an industry which is contracting by 10 per cent are, by definition, wanted where they are just as much as ever they were, it seems a little hard that their wages should be held back by the necessity of inducing those who are now superfluous to leave. In these conditions, it may well be true that less injury would be done to every-body, if the necessary contraction were effected by a temporary closing of the door to new recruitment in the declining industry: that is, if it were made a statutory offense for any person not already connected with the overstocked industry to take employment in it, until the surplus had been cleared by the merciful working of "natural wastage." The unregulated inflow into certain

industries has been one of the worst disorders of our dis-
orderly economic system in the past. Building has been
one of the greatest sufferers (or should one say "offenders"?) in this respect. Between 1924 and 1938 the
number of insured workers in that industry increased from
680,000 to 1,050,000; yet the percentage registered as unemployed was nearly 50 per cent higher in the latter than
in the former year. A high proportion of the new recruits
must thus have become, not builders, but unemployed
builders. Even if this particular scandal is overcome by
the conquest of unemployment, the problem of reduc-
ing the strength of a declining industry (and there must
be contractions as well as expansions in a progressive
world of changing needs and changing techniques) with
a minimum of hardship is not easily solved by the use of
economic incentives alone.

This is indeed one of the few cases where legal sanctions may actually work more kindly than economic inducements. To close the doors of an industry or profession
against people who have never been accustomed to pass
those doors is a very small infringement of freedom—at
least in a world of full employment in which there are
plenty of other places to which to go. Such prohibitions
are, moreover, likely only to be occasional and temporary:
and they need not, and should not, interfere with complete freedom of choice of *job* for all those who are eligible
for employment in the industry at all. In the event of a
contraction of the mining industry, it may be necessary
to make an order forbidding anyone who has not previously been a miner from taking a job in the mines. But
this has nothing to do with the right of those who are
and have been miners to sign on at whichever they like

best of the pits that have vacancies. It ought, perhaps, to be added that no persons interested either as employers or as employees in a particular industry or occupation ought ever to have power of themselves alone to impose legal restrictions on recruitment to that industry or occupation.

Smooth distribution of labor in a planned economy would also be facilitated by one further measure, which might be counted a small curtailment of freedom; that is, compulsory notification of all engagements (and terminations of engagements) to the Employment Exchanges. In this way the public authorities concerned with planning would be fully informed of what was going on in the labor market. Without this information, it would be very difficult, accurately, to manage the adjustment of pay and prospects necessary to get workers where they were wanted. Compulsory notification of engagements, it should, however, be added, means only just what it says—notification of *engagements*, not compulsory registration of workers available for employment or vacancies offered by employers. It is not always appreciated that these additional measures, innocent though they look, would necessarily involve industrial conscription. For compulsory registration for employment is only practicable, if we have a firm definition of who is to be registered, on the one hand, and an equally precise definition, on the other hand, of when a vacancy is, and when it is not, so to speak, a vacancy. The first is impossible, unless the law and not the individuals concerned, decides who is in the labor market and who is not. Persons legally liable to register are by definition legally liable to offer themselves for employment: that is to say, they are subject to industrial conscription. Without powers of conscription, compulsory registration of workers must become farcical, since anybody can truthfully say that he is undecided in his own mind whether to look for a job or not: it depends on what sort of a job turns up, or on a number of personal and domestic factors. Similarly, compulsory notification of vacancies is impossible, because an employer may in practice only make an opening when he sees a likely looking man, instead of looking for someone to fill a pre-existing vacancy.

Compulsory notification of engagements is open to no such objections. If, however, the beginning and ending of all contracts of employment had to be notified to the Exchanges, it is likely that both employers and workers would increasingly use the Exchange of their own accord, as a means of finding one another; so that the percentage of engagements actually effected through, as distinct from notified to, the Exchanges would increase. This, too, should help to get people sorted out into suitable jobs quickly and smoothly through the ordinary machinery of the labor market. But the utmost legal obligation that can be imposed, consistently with free choice of occupation, is the obligation to tell the Exchanges whom you have dismissed or engaged, or what job you have accepted or relinquished.

Free choice of employment is, of course, itself, just as much as freedom of consumption, dependent upon the game being played according to the rules. The most important rule here is that people should be willing to move from job to job as the demands of industry require, in response to what we have called the method of inducement. An inert and sluggish public might have to be kicked around, where a community of active and enterprising folk would be adaptable and mobile enough to suit the demands of any reasonable economic plan. Unfortunately, we know very little indeed from experience about our own probable behavior in this respect in the kind of conditions which we hope to see after the war. Nearly all inferences from pre-war mobility are invalidated by the distorting effects of unemployment. In pre-war conditions the *negative* inducement responsible for getting people away from where there was no sale for their labor was a combination of reduced pay and greatly increased risk of unemployment, with unemployment the predominating partner: the *positive* inducement to attract them elsewhere was, as a rule, a prospect of somewhat better pay with considerably greater chances, but still no security, of employment. There can be little doubt that the fact, or the risk, of unemployment has done much more to make people stick to the job that they have got, or look for the job that they haven't, than have any nice calculations about probable earnings. But it is by no means clear *in which direction* the factor of unemployment operates in any particular case. A man who is already out of work has, certainly, the strongest possible inducement to look for another job in his own, or in some other, occupation or industry: on the other hand, the limited resources of the unemployed make it difficult for them to look for work far afield. Again, the presence of heavy unemployment in your own trade, or even of quite moderate unemployment in some other district or industry, to which you might otherwise be attracted by the prospect of better pay and conditions, is likely to encourage an attitude of extreme caution: where all is so uncertain, those who can will hang on to their jobs while they can, whatever the drawbacks.

The one reasonably certain inference that can be drawn from experience in this context is that people are more ready to change their job, or their occupation, or to move from one industry to another, provided that they do not also have to move their homes. This is certainly in accord with what one would expect, and it is also borne out by the facts. Industrial is much greater than geographical, mobility, at least in this country. This has an important moral, as Sir William Beveridge has pointed out,[2] for planners. For it means that the job of matching labor supply with production programs is likely to be simplified if care is taken about the location of industries. It will, therefore, generally be wiser (where this is physically possible) to take the work to the workers, rather than to expect the workers to take themselves to the work.

If free choice of employment is compatible only with planned production, provided that the working population is sufficiently mobile, it is also only practicable provided that mobility does not run mad. It is all guesswork, but I am myself inclined to think that when the fear of unemployment is removed, excessive mobility, particularly between job and job (as distinct from movement from one occupation or industry to another) is more to be feared than undue sluggishness. This has certainly been the case in Soviet Russia; but there may have been special factors there which would not be repeated in our more mature industrialism—such as the excitement and instability of people who are just entering industry for the first time, and the greater mobility of a population which contains

2. *Full Employment in a Free Society.*

a high proportion of young people. Excessive mobility is particularly to be expected in the years when we are first tasting the joy of freedom from industrial direction, without fear of unemployment. Even if the power of compulsory direction is retained during the actual switch from war to peace production, those whose mobility has long been bound, first by economic compulsion, and then by statutory rule, may be eager to take deep draughts at their new freedom to exchange one job for another on comparatively trivial grounds. If, in fact, these fears prove to be well-founded, then we shall be driven (like the Russians) to control mobility by imposing economic penalties, less harsh and wasteful than unemployment, upon the incurably restless: this is discussed below in the section that follows. But we are not even then thrown back upon conscription or direction, enforced by legal sanctions.

The final condition for preserving free choice of employment where economic priorities are deliberately determined is implicit in all that has been said above: it is that rates of pay should be actually adaptable to the demand for labor necessary to fulfill any plans. It is useless to say that variations in wages (upwards and downwards) are to be the stimulus which will attract workers into jobs here, and repel them from jobs there, if the necessary adjustments upwards and downwards are then not made. This raises the whole issue of the determination of wages under planning. Since this issue involves a distinct and most important group of freedoms—those concerned with the right to strike, and the right to bargain about wages—it is discussed in the next chapter in connection with these particular liberties.

II

We must now return to the question whether free choice of employment needs to be restricted by any economic or near-economic sanctions. The most powerful restriction of all—the fear that if you lose or refuse one job it may be ever so long before another one comes along, and that in the meantime you will have no income—is of course greatly enfeebled, as soon as we postulate that vacancies exceed applicants, instead of vice versa. But it has also been softened in a world of underemployment by the introduction of unemployment insurance or relief. It is to this experience that we must look for enlightenment, as to the proper limits of choice of employment in an economy which does not leave its production programs and problems of labor supply to settle themselves.

Our present Unemployment Insurance regulations provide that a worker who leaves his job voluntarily, or is dismissed for misconduct, or refuses "suitable" employment, is liable to total deprivation of insurance benefit for a period not exceeding six weeks. The definition "suitable" is naturally rather a delicate matter. In practice, this qualification has been rigidly interpreted so as to prevent unemployed persons from being deprived of benefit merely because they refuse to accept jobs at less than their standard rate (another treacherous term) of wages, or because they will not act as strike breakers. Further, "suitable" employment normally means employment in your own trade, except in the case of those who have been out of work for a considerable period. Courts of Referees have power to stop the benefit of unemployed

persons who, after a long spell of unemployment, are not
willing to try their hand at work to which they have not
previously been accustomed. There is, moreover, an over-
all limit to the number of weeks during which benefit
may be drawn consecutively; and the Government have
announced their intention of retaining this limit in the
all-in social insurance scheme which it is proposed to
introduce after the war. Taken together, these regulations
represent the latest design for meeting the twin difficulties
of what may be called frivolous mobility on the one hand,
and obstinate immobility on the other. Neither of these
difficulties will be automatically resolved by full employment. The first, as has already been suggested, may actually be aggravated; and, as for the second, we have to
recognize that while intelligent planning may provide
more than enough jobs of one sort or another, only the
most *un*intelligent planning could guarantee, in a dynamic
economy, that everybody could retain the same type of
employment throughout his working life.

Now, while the disabilities imposed by these regulations are rightly classified as economic, rather than legal,
restrictions on completely free choice of employment, yet
the strictly economic penalty imposed is itself something
of a façade. For while the Unemployment Insurance Acts
faithfully deprive both the frivolously mobile and the
sluggish immobile of their insurance benefit, the Assistance
Board stands in the background, ready to come to the
rescue of any cases of hardship that result from this deprivation. A man who is deprived of unemployment benefit,
on the ground, for example, of his having discharged
himself from his job, may be no worse off financially than
a neighbor whose unemployment is entirely involuntary:

it is not indeed unknown for him to be a shilling or two *better* off. For, if the voluntarily unemployed has no other means of support for himself and his family, the Assistance Board will maintain him on a prescribed scale—which may compare quite favorably with insurance benefit. The essential difference between insurance and assistance is not the amount payable in each case, but the fact that assistance is dependent on proof of need, and therefore upon a means test which is often, rightly or wrongly, felt to be humiliating.

We have, in fact, already abandoned the strict Pauline principle that he that will not work, neither shall he eat—even for the working classes to whom alone it was ever seriously applied. Instead, we have substituted the principle: he that will not work, neither shall he eat very well, or without a lot of fuss. This is the rule that now obtains in every sense of the phrase "will not work," known to the Unemployment Insurance Acts and Regulations. It covers those who are discharged for misconduct, those who have left voluntarily, and those whose idea of suitable work, even after a long period of unemployment, does not square with the view taken by a Court of Referees or by the Umpire. But it is hardly accurate to say that free choice of employment is limited by strictly *economic* compulsions, when he that will not work has a good chance of eating quite as well as he that will, but cannot.

The present position seems, indeed, to be resolving itself into something like this. We have not yet admitted the claim of any citizen (except a property-owner) to live *at all comfortably* at the expense of others while refusing to do any work at all, or at least any work other than that which suits his own special fancy. On the other hand we are not prepared actually to allow anybody to starve. We compromise uneasily by restricting the income payable as of right to *any* unemployed person, even the potentially most industrious, to a very low level indeed— just so as to be on the safe side. In the year 1944 the Government, indeed, expressly rejected the principle that unemployment insurance benefit for the involuntarily unemployed should be adequate for subsistence. Yet meantime we do, in fact, support even the most incorrigible idler—relying on his presumed objection to a means test, rather than upon any difference between the living standards of the idle and the industrious—to express our disapproval of his idleness. The difference between the economic standard of the voluntarily and the involuntarily unemployed is, therefore, *necessarily* very narrow—so long as we leave the latter enough to live upon, and are afraid to give the former much more.

This compromise looks increasingly grotesque and improper in the light of such crystallization of current social standards as the Atlantic Charter and the Four Freedoms. Eventually we shall, I think, have to accept these statements at their face value, and to interpret freedom from want as freedom from want, not as freedom from want for the industrious, the stable, and the adaptable. We are, in fact, constantly driven by pressure of public sentiment, though very slowly, along that road. The introduction of social insurance, the separation of unemployment assistance from public assistance, and the proposed final abolition of all the old poor law machinery —every one of these changes is a reluctant admission that he who cannot or will not work shall, nevertheless, eat. Gingerly levering up standards at the bottom, however, only creates fresh troubles if economic pressure is to play any part in determining choice of employer. For any provision for the voluntarily unemployed, which is not so mean as to be absolutely penal, treads hard upon the heels of the meager and limited benefits payable to those whose unemployment is in no sense of their own making. In that case, the opportunity for economic discrimination between the worker who throws up, and the worker who is thrown out of, his job, grows smaller and smaller; and with it shrinks also the opportunity for discriminating between refusal of "suitable" and of "unsuitable" employment.

In effect, the only way to combine universal freedom from want with the use of strictly economic sanctions against excessive or deficient mobility is to *widen* the margin between the minimum subsistence paid in all cases even of voluntary unemployment, and the normal insurance benefit payable as of right to the "genuinely" unemployed, by *pushing the latter generously upwards*. Then, if completely free choice of employment threatened to produce a chaotic or inappropriate distribution of labor, or reckless scurrying from job to job, or prevented the translation of paper plans into actual performance, there would be scope for correcting these mistakes by the use of effective and positive economic inducements. The unduly mobile and the unduly conservative who declined suitable employment could then suffer deductions from their rates of unemployment benefit without being flung into grievous want.

Any deductions from unemployment pay which are intended as a sanction to enforce acceptance of suitable employment should, moreover, logically, be deductions in amount and not limitations in time. They should replace both the total disqualification from insurance benefit now imposed for six weeks upon those who leave voluntarily or through their own misconduct, and the withdrawal of benefit from those who, after a "reasonable" time, refuse to take employment, or training for employment, in occupations other than those to which they have been accustomed. Otherwise we shall be back again in the old dilemma that, if a person is completely deprived of all income from one source, it stands to reason that he must get something to live upon from somewhere else. In the many cases where friends, relations, or savings are not enough, "somewhere else" can only mean some other public fund; and that will once more make nonsense of our economic sanctions. Both the insufficiently and the excessively mobile should, in short, pay for their peculiarities by descending from a subsistence-plus to a subsistence income; but on that lower level they should be left unmolested until they are actually in work again.

Along these lines, we may sooner or later find a happy and civilized solution of the present contradiction in which we are afraid to let anyone starve, and at the same time afraid wholly to forego the threat of starvation. In that event, the revised Pauline doctrine, adapted to the standards of a more lavishly provided age, would read: He that will not work shall eat sufficiently and without dishonor; but he that is willing to work shall at all times, whether actually working or not, enjoy greater abundance. Such a policy implies, however, a bold confidence both that fear of grievous want is a poor and ineffective incentive; and that in a free and generous society, where opportunity is abundant, the idle, the capricious and the unadaptable are not likely to be a major social problem.

CHAPTER VII

The Freedom of the Producer

II. FREEDOM OF COLLECTIVE BARGAINING

O F ALL the possible points of conflict between conscious planning of priorities and traditional freedoms, the regulation of wages is likely to prove the most
stormy. Successful planning may indeed be dependent here
upon deep changes in social attitudes. For if certain jobs
are in fact to be done, it is obvious that there cannot *both*
be complete freedom to choose and to refuse your job,
and equal freedom to choose and to refuse the wages that
you are to be paid; except in the sense that free choice
of employment necessarily implies the right to turn a job
down on the ground that the wages offered are insuffi-
cient. Where, however, as in this country, the practice
of independent collective bargaining is well established,
organized workers are accustomed to claim much more
than this. They expect the rates of wages payable in
different trades and occupations to be fixed by a process
of free bargaining between the employers and workers
in which nobody else has meddled.

It is this claim which is likely to make difficulties. For
when we are relying on wage adjustments to match the
demand and supply in the labor market, what guarantee
can we have, under a system of free bargaining, that those

adjustments will in fact be made? Suppose, for example, that a large-scale building program is planned: the first step necessary is then to make a guess (it will never be more than a guess, continually modified by trial-and-error experience) at the rates of pay at which it will be possible to recruit the right grades of workers in the right places. If however, the public authorities, or the contractors to whom the actual building work may have been handed over, are bidding against other employers in an uncontrolled labor market, all these guesses may be thrown out by events in that market. Employers on low priority work may, by the offer of better rates, steal the workers on whom the Government was relying to carry out its own plans. That these possibilities are not imaginary is plain enough from experience of what happened in the early stages of the war; experience which is particularly likely to recur whenever unemployment is negligible. First attempts to deal with the war-time problem were rather half-hearted, and took the form of Control of Engagement Orders, restricting the freedom of employers to take on workers without official permission. It was not until general industrial direction firmly abolished free choice of employment altogether that the Government felt really confident of being able to make a safe and happy marriage between labor supply and production plans.

Nor can it be said that these difficulties will arise only where the scope of planning is relatively restricted. It is not just a question of possible competition between Government and private firms for the services of the same workpeople. Even if we assume such complete public control of the economic pattern as has been established in Russia, the problem is exactly the same. If the plans demand more engineers and fewer carpenters, and nobody is to be conscripted out of carpentering into engineering, there must be appropriate adjustments of engineers' and carpenters' wages. But if the engineers and carpenters claim the right to determine these rates by independent collective bargaining in which they are equal partners with their particular employers, there can be no security that the answer will come out right in terms of the demands of the Government's plans. There is of course no reason why the Government, or the directorate of particular industries, should not enter into *discussion* with Trade Union representatives of workers (as they do in Russia) before fixing or changing wage rates. But if the plans are to be fulfilled, the discussion must be conducted on terms which guarantee that the employing side is bound in the last resort to win every time: which is not what is generally understood in this country by free collective bargaining.

In effect this means that conscious determination of production priorities implies also conscious regulation of relative wage rates. There must in fact be a plan for wages; and this planning of wage rates must, indeed, extend not only as far as the planning of production, but farther. The wages payable in industries and firms producing independently for the market (unless the scale of these is quite insignificant) must march in step with those paid on Government-sponsored production programs— otherwise we run into the dangers, already mentioned, of competitive bidding for labor. With a free choice of employment, every pattern of production implies a corresponding pattern of wages. We are thus faced with a double task: that of designing the wage pattern correctly, and that of transferring it from paper to practice.

This is something which has never been attempted under any of the present methods by which wages are fixed—outside the U.S.S.R. Take, first, the traditional methods of collective bargaining between employers and Trade Unions. This is invariably conducted in a piecemeal way; and the pieces have, moreover, been assorted by historical processes that are quite irrelevant to any coherent picture of relative wages. Wage negotiations are conducted by particular Trade Unions sitting down with particular Employers' Associations. What group a particular Trade Union represents is determined by these irrelevant historical processes. Unions amalgamate when their members think that they will get more through one big organization than in several smaller ones; new Unions are founded, or broken off from those already formed, when a body of workers think that under the existing set-up they are not getting as much as they might. So we have the familiar jumble of Unions covering and negotiating wages for a single craft, a whole industry, or a miscellany of occupations and industries; as well as the similar confusion of national Unions, regional Unions and Unions that cover only a single city.

In these conditions it would indeed be remarkable if the rates of wages earned in different occupations were spontaneously to shape themselves into any coherent or rational picture. The Trade Unions have no plan for wages; each of a thousand and more separate Unions is doing the best it can for its members according to its lights. The power of the Trades Union Congress to make its affiliated Unions toe the line in wage policy is no greater than the power of the League of Nations over its constituent states; and for much the same reason. The Trades Union Congress, like the League of Nations, shows no sign of seriously *wanting* effective power. The Congress, and the General Council, acting as the executive body between Congresses, are composed of representatives of separate Unions meeting together primarily as the spokesmen of their own societies: their first loyalty is not inside, but outside, the Congress or Council Chambers, not to Transport House, but each to his own particular society up and down the country. The duties of the Trades Union Congress are thus consultative and advisory: every wage claim and every strike must be initiated and approved by the Union on behalf of whose members it is made. Nor have we any evidence that the consultation and advice offered by the central body are informed by a desire to shape relative wages into some considered and rationally defensible plan. Just as it is the business of each Union to get the best conditions that it can for its members (for that after all is what the members subscribe for), so it is the business of the Trades Union Congress General Council to advise each Union how best to promote the welfare of its particular members. Reference to other societies will only come into the picture in so far as a claim by, say, the miners might, for tactical reasons, help or hinder a claim by the engineers.

What is true of the Unions is, of course, no less true of employers. Bargaining is sectional on both sides of the table. One party wishes to get as much, and the other party wishes, broadly speaking, to pay, as little as possible. But neither is thinking of anybody but himself. This is no ground for condemnation. The officials of a

Union of employers or employees are expressly paid, and
the committees expressly elected, for the purpose of looking after the interests of their members. They are no more
to be blamed if they do this job, and this job only, than a
lawyer engaged for the defense is to be blamed if he
does not urge upon the Court the social importance of
imposing an adequate penalty upon his client. This point
is often overlooked in criticisms which are light-heartedly
made upon "the anti-social" policy of Trade Unions. It
is in fact the business of a Union to be anti-social: the
members would have a just grievance if their officials and
committees ceased to put sectional interests first. The same
is true of all societies founded to promote, or to protect,
any interest which is liable to come into conflict with the
interests of others; and it is difficult to think of interests
which are not so liable; though the conflicts may not
always be as severe or constant as the conflict between,
say, the claim of the doctors to exclude alien practitioners,
and the claim of the public for more and better medical
services. Societies for the preservation of rural England
conflict with speculative builders, and even the ornitholo-
gists (as witness the film *Tawny Pipit*) may conflict with
the military. Blame for the consequences of the anti-social
policies of sectional organizations like Trade Unions lies,
not upon the societies themselves, but upon our practice
of allowing issues by which many parties are affected to be
settled by one or two of those parties alone. Indeed, in
so complex a community as ours, these sectional societies
are doing an important job in looking after interests which
might easily be overridden or neglected, if there were no
such organized channel through which their claims might
be heard. The partisan attitude of counsel for the prosecu-

tion and counsel for the defense is useful and proper as long as cases are settled by judge and jury. But such an attitude would be disastrous if disputes at law were left to the mercies of battle or bargain between the lawyers on each side.

Where wages are settled by free collective bargaining, such factors as the strength, or degree of monopoly, enjoyed by the organizations on both sides, together with the skill of the negotiators, must necessarily play a big part in pushing rates up here, or down there. These influences will themselves operate within the limits of a certain social and economic environment (the most powerful Union or the cleverest negotiator cannot perform miracles); and that environment will in turn be shaped, on the one hand, by external economic circumstances like the rise and fall of demand for particular products, or the coming and going of different techniques of production, and, on the other hand, by the immense weight of conservatism which overhangs all our notions of what different skills and types of work ought to be paid. None of this has anything to do with the rational regulation of wages in accordance with the labor demands of a determinate production plan.

The alternatives to free collective bargaining already in use—and increasingly used—are statutory determination of wages, or some kind of industrial arbitration. Apart from special war-time legislation, the wages of workers in the Trade Board trades, and of some road transport and catering workers are already fixed by the former method: arbitration is increasingly used where the parties cannot of themselves agree, and is the normal method of wage-fixing in war conditions. As a rule both wage-fixing bodies with statutory powers and arbitration tribunals include "impartial" persons, who are neither parties to the issue, nor representatives of any employers' or workers' organizations. Some arbitrations (but not usually those involving large questions of substance, as distinct from interpretation of agreements already made) are conducted by "impartial" persons alone: more commonly these judicial elements are flanked by representatives of the employers and employed who may or may not be attached (in the statutory bodies they usually are, and in the arbitration tribunals they usually are not) to the particular trade or industry whose claim is being heard. The essential difference between the statutory bodies and the arbitrators are, first, that the former have, and the latter have not, powers of initiative: and, second, that any decisions made are enforced by quite different types of sanction in the two cases. (This point is discussed later.) [1] It should be added that the arbitrator's business is in theory anyhow to fix *standard* rates, while that of a Trade Board or Agricultural Wages Board is to fix minima. This difference is not, however, very important in practice.

These impartial persons clearly hold a key position. But their lot, like the policeman's, is not, I fear, a very happy one. As a rule they are given no instructions as to principles; and except for a few rare indiscretions,[2] they are

1. See pp. 114-21.
2. As, for instance the famous pronouncement of the Industrial Court in March 1920:—
"During the war period, when commercial conditions were disturbed or in abeyance, the cost of living was an important factor in determining wages. Now that the markets are again open it appears to the Court that an alteration in the cost of living does not in itself necessarily warrant any corresponding alteration in wages. The remuneration of the various classes of workpeople should, in

generally too cautious voluntarily to admit to any principles of their own. Where guidance is given, it does not seem to be framed in a way that is likely to give much practical help: see, for instance, the instructions given to the Agricultural Wages Committees under the Act of 1924 which imposes the duty of, "as far as practicable," securing for "able-bodied men such wages as ... are adequate to promote efficiency, and to enable a man in an ordinary case to maintain himself and his family in accordance with such standard of comfort as may be reasonable in relation to the nature of his occupation."

At present, therefore, the "impartial" arbitrator has generally to fumble about for himself. In practice it looks as if there were three grounds for wage changes which he generally finds impressive. The first is evidence of a rise in the cost of living: the second is the argument that the wages of some other group doing work comparable to that of the claimants have been raised; and the third is the plea that the prosperity of an industry justifies an increase of wages to the workers employed in it, or, conversely, that an industry is so unprosperous that existing wage levels cannot be maintained. To these three arguments we should perhaps add one other, which has been chiefly prominent in the statutory wage-fixing bodies, viz.: the claim that current wage rates are exceptionally low, and that it is impossible to live upon them. I mention this last

---

ordinary circumstances, depend on the value of the work done, and the value of the work done depends on the state of the market, and the demand for the products of the workshop."

As a general rule, however, the Court has taken the view that, on such large issues of principle as those raised in the foregoing sentences, silence is the better part of valor.

argument with greater hesitation, because practically
everybody who asks for higher wages uses the plea that
it is impossible to live on what he is now getting. Everywhere, however, except at the very bottom, this simply
means that it is impossible to live on present wages at a
standard of living which is itself determined by reference
to the standards of other people in other groups. Hence,
except at the lowest levels of all, the complaint that one
cannot live on one's wages boils down to a claim that
these wages are out of step with those of other people, and
is therefore really only a special variety of our second
argument.

The effect of the first two of these arguments is over-
whelmingly conservative. If wages are adjusted to suit
changes in the cost of living, the result is to keep everybody's real standard exactly where it was before. Arbitrators are quite unnecessary for this job, which could be
better done by arithmetic. If, again, A's wages are to be
increased or cut to correspond with changes in the wages
earned by B, though there may be ups and downs in absolute standards, the effect will be to keep everybody in
the same *relative* position as before. The only door
through which change that is both absolute and relative
can enter is by way of variations in the prosperity of an
industry; and, in a less degree, by leveling up at the
bottom. More and more, however, variations of prosperity
are being smoothed out by Government subsidies and protection for the unfortunate; and, more and more, public
opinion rebels against the idea that people's absolute or
relative wage position should be, anyhow *un*favorably, affected by circumstances which are in no way of their own
making. Arguments from prosperity are moreover gener-

ally ruled out or heavily discounted in the growing sphere of national and local public enterprise.

The upshot of this is that the general effect of arbitration and statutory wage fixing is heavily conservative. These mechanisms increase the rigidity of wage standards, both relatively and absolutely. There is another reason for this also. People's attitude toward questions of wage policy is strongly colored by ethical considerations: it is not, we say, "fair" that library assistants should earn less than shorthand typists. The continual use of terms like "fair," however, is quite subjective: no commonly accepted ethical pattern can be implied. The wretched arbitrator, who is charged with the duty of acting "fairly and impartially" is thus required to show these qualities in circumstances in which they have no meaning; for there can be no such thing as fairness or impartiality except in terms of an accepted code. No one can be impartial in a vacuum. One can only umpire at cricket because there are rules, or at a boxing match so long as certain blows, like those below the belt, are forbidden. Where, therefore, as in wage determinations, there are no rules and no code, the only possible interpretation of impartiality is conservatism. Since people have accepted the *status quo,* they probably will continue to do so: impartiality then consists in restoring this *status quo* in any cases in which it happens to have been disturbed. It should be remembered too that arbitrators, in particular, are entirely dependent upon the goodwill of their clients. No Union need go to arbitration in time of peace if it does not want to; and no Union can compel a recalcitrant employers' organization to go to arbitration.

All this has a significant bearing on the problem of wage determination, in circumstances in which economic priorities are deliberately determined, but industrial conscription is ruled out. What it means is that all the familiar methods of adjusting wages are quite inappropriate to the demands of economic planning. If we retain completely free collective bargaining, we should have somehow to induce a quite revolutionary change in the attitude of the parties to those bargains. It would, moreover, be a change which would completely do away with bargaining in the present sense of a tussle of economic strength and wits; and which would do violence to the fundamental *raison d' être* of the organizations which now make these bargains. Trade Unions, and their counterparts on the employers' side, exist, as we have said, to get all they can for their members. They would be turned upside down and inside out, if they renounced this function in favor of the task of helping to regulate wages and conditions of employment in such a way as to match labor supply with the requirements of public plans.

Conceivably, since freedom of collective bargaining is much cherished in this country, the best way of retaining this freedom, as the scope of economic planning extends, would be frankly to invite the co-operation of the Unions in their own metamorphosis in this way. The success of any such plan (which looks impossible on paper) would be entirely dependent upon a large dose of goodwill, commonsense and understanding. It would be one of those cases in which a freedom was retained on condition that it was exercised with exceptional discretion. Not all plans that look impossible on paper are unworkable in practice.

On paper it is impossible that the British Commonwealth, at least since the statute of Westminster, should
have hung together as long as it has. But it has.

The alternative is to make much more general use of
arbitration. Such a step would again mean a revolutionary
change of attitude and policy—this time on the part of
arbitrators. But this might be very welcome. For whereas
a Trade Union which is asked to negotiate, not in order to
get the best possible terms for its members, but so as to
keep wages in harmony with some predetermined pattern,
finds the sense knocked out of its position, an arbitrator
might well find that such guidance would for the first time
put sense into his. Under a system of wage regulation by
public authorities, the Trade Unions could, moreover, still
retain their traditional, indeed their proper, role of advocates. The final decision would necessarily rest, when there
was dispute, with the impartial persons, whose function
would then approximate to that of judge or jury in the
courts; and the Unions' business would be to see that no
factor affecting the interest of their clients had been overlooked in the process by which this decision was reached.

Any suggestion that wage-rates should generally be
fixed by public bodies immediately raises once more the
question of sanctions. And here I think we have to face
the fact that any conceivable sanction is bound to do violence to deeply cherished liberties. At present, Trade
Boards and the wage boards in agriculture, catering and
road transport exercise a legal sanction. Those employers
who fail to pay at least the prescribed rates are liable to
criminal penalties; and the worker has also a civil right
to arrears due. This precedent has, however, no relevance
to our present problem, since these bodies are concerned

only to fix *minima*. If movements of relative wages are to
be the main instrument for matching the supply of labor
with the demands of definite plans, then payment of
wages above, as well as below, the prescribed rates may
throw production programs out of gear. Especially in conditions of full employment, the risk of counter-bidding for
labor by employers whose business ranks low on the plans,
against those with higher priority, may, as we have seen,
be quite serious. Such bidding will, moreover, be encour-
aged if the fraternization between the employers' organizations and the Unions in particular industries, of
which there have been significant hints during the war,
should continue when the war is over. The Unions' traditional threats of fire and slaughter against the capitalist
classes are not always to be taken at their full face value.
There are plenty of Trade Union leaders quick enough to
see that richer prizes may be won by marching hand-in-
hand with employers to exploit monopolistic positions
(and the monopolies favored by war have a way of linger-
ing on into peace), than can ever be realized by the old-
fashioned policy of milking your employer all you can.
Such an alignment between Unions and employers, might,
moreover, not only threaten the pattern of relative wages
necessary to effective planning: it might also be the beginning of a general process of competitive bidding and
counter-bidding of money wages upwards, which could
only be sustained by a corresponding inflation of prices,
and would thus defeat its own ends. These difficulties
have only been avoided (as far as they have) during the
war period of full employment, because, on the one hand,
both employers and Unions are restrained by patriotic
motives from exploiting the full strength of their position;

while on the other hand, industrial direction firmly controls the distribution of labor.

Should such tactics be employed, by what sanction could a planned pattern of wage rates be enforced? Any proposal either that employers who pay, or that workers who take, wages in excess of the rates prescribed should be liable to penalties, comparable to those now imposed on employers who violate minimum wage laws, would be an unthinkably severe reduction of traditional liberties. In some quarters the apparently less drastic method of prohibiting by law *collective* defiance, through strikes and lockouts, of wage determinations might find more favor; but to the whole Trade Union movement this would be extreme tyranny. Moreover, even apart from the rights and the wrongs of such a policy, any discrimination between legal and illegal strikes raises some tricky practical issues. In any illegal strike the offending persons are the strikers. A striker is a person who leaves his work, with or without notice, in company with a large number of his colleagues. This means, however, that the offense of being a striker is an exceedingly difficult one to prove. For all that an individual striker has done is to absent himself from work; he can, if he likes, assert that this had nothing to do with the fact that several thousand other people also absented themselves on the same day: nobody is more surprised than he to hear of such a coincidence! It follows, therefore, that measures to punish illegal strikes are in practice directed, not against individual strikers, but against the persons and organizations who incite others to strike. The Trade Union Act of 1927, which first introduced this distinction between the legal and the illegal strike, recognized the impossibility of proving a case against the individual striker. No one is subject to any penalty under this law for the act of striking; but it is a criminal offense to organize an illegal strike, or to encourage others to join the strikers; and Unions responsible for calling illegal strikes become also liable at civil law for damages to employers or others to whom the strike has caused loss or injury, though in a legal strike they would be immune from such actions. The result of this is that the only penalties which can be used against illegal strikes are by their very nature such as will cripple the Unions in the exercise of their perfectly legal and proper functions also. If the Executive Committee and officers of a Union have gone to prison for calling an illegal strike, and the funds of the Union have been sequestrated for damages, the Union is out of action as an instrument for defending the legitimate and proper interests of its members. This no doubt partly explains the extreme hostility of the Trade Union movement to the suggestion that any kind of strike should be outlawed. For this necessity of visiting the sins of the striker upon the Union behind him has nothing to do with the particular grounds on which a strike may be judged illegal. At present, apart from war legislation, the only strikes which are prohibited by law are "sympathetic" and "political" strikes—that is, those which are not concerned with the "conditions of employment in the trade or industry in which the strikers are engaged"—and then only if the strike is "designed to coerce the Government, either directly, or indirectly, by causing hardship to the community." But the position would be just the same if strikes against arbitration decisions were made illegal. Only where workers are liable to industrial conscription can proceedings be taken against the actual strikers. For in these conditions it is an offense to stay away from work anyhow, whether alone, or in company.

The long and the short of it is, then, that planned production implies either compulsory industrial direction or a planned wage structure. Yet there is no sanction by which a given pattern of relative wages can be enforced which does not involve encroachments on existing liberties such as would widely be thought to be intolerable. I do not think that we should underestimate the seriousness of this dilemma. The Russians have resolved it, apparently, by withholding the right of free collective bargaining as we understand this. It is true that discussions take place between the representatives of Soviet Trade Unions and of industrial managements which result in a "collective agreement." But these negotiations are concerned, it seems, with the allocation as between various grades and skills of a planned total wage fund for each industry; which is a very different matter from starting with a clean sheet and trying to get what you can, raising your own total, if necessary, at the expense of the real wages earned in other industries. Moreover, the Soviet Trade Unions, which have for practical purposes grown up under the revolutionary régime, and are indeed its creations if not its creatures, have no such background of independence as have ours. It is likely that they could accept without difficulty the view that their job was to negotiate such rates and conditions as would in fact harmonize the distribution of labor with the requirements of the plans. The British Unions might, indeed, as I have suggested, be converted to that attitude; but the Russians have the advantage of having been born in the faith. And in the last resort the Soviet Unions and the Soviet workers have not in fact any right to strike comparable with that jealously guarded by our own Trade Union movement.

Ardent admirers of the Soviet regime usually parry this issue, with the retort that the right to strike has no relevance in the U.S.S.R., since no Soviet worker would want or need to strike. This answer is not, perhaps, as silly as it appears on the face of it. No one except those directly concerned can, of course, know whether people who are not free to strike wish to do so or not. Nevertheless it may well be true that our best chance lies in the hope that the wish to disturb a national wage structure will be absent. Certainly it is a fact that where arbitration has in the past been voluntarily accepted, the resulting decisions, unsupported by either legal or economic sanctions, have, in the great majority of cases, been loyally accepted. It may or may not also be true that extensive use of compulsory arbitration during the war will have fostered the view that the determination of wages is in every case as much a matter of public policy as a private bargain of concern only to directly interested parties. The conservative tendency of arbitrations will be a handicap here; for the future of wage-fixing bodies will inevitably be inferred from their past, and it will be difficult to make due allowance for the difference between arbitration by rational principle and arbitration in a void. Even so, however, I think it likely that the doctrine that planned production implies planned wages will find readier acceptance, if it becomes the rule for wages to be fixed by public authorities, than if we rely on a changed spirit in collective bargaining. It is sometimes possible sincerely to welcome and to co-operate in changes proposed by others which it would have been difficult to advocate warmly on one's own initiative. In practice, a great deal will certainly depend on the use made of freedom of collective bargaining in the early post-war years when we may anticipate release from the compulsory arbitration to which we are now subject. If, in fact, this freedom is then exercised with understanding and discretion, so that relative wages are well adapted to the demands of planned production, then planning, free choice of employment, and free collective bargaining may well march together.

We need to remember, too, that good pay and prospects cannot influence the actions of people who have never heard anything about them. Any orderly system of regulating wages in accordance with the labor requirements of production plans needs to be supported by clear and abundant publicity as to what opportunities are available where. We may well underestimate the effect, in the post-war world, of merely *telling* people where their services are wanted. After all, they never *have* been told. Before the war we were left to apply at the vacancy counter at the Exchange, or to plow our way through advertisement columns, or to pick up a job where a relation or neighbor could speak for us—with no authoritative guidance whatever as to the fields in which substantial and lasting expansion was to be expected. It may well turn out in practice that sensible and intelligible advice proves a close second to adjustment of wages, as an instrument for directing labor without resort to compulsion.

On the most pessimistic assumption that all these devices fail, the price of planning must be either compulsory industrial direction or compulsory arbitration backed by legal sanctions. If it comes to that, compulsory arbitration is much to be preferred to industrial direction. To the individual, compulsory arbitration means that his wages are fixed not by a bargain between his Union and his employers, but by "neutral persons" who have listened to the arguments of these two parties. In neither case does he personally have much say in the matter; and he may even persuade himself that he is likely to do as well in the one case as in the other. Standard rates of wages are not the result of his own decisions. But free choice of employment is a much more personal matter. You either take a job or you don't: the decision is your own. Under industrial direction freedom to make this active personal decision is entirely destroyed.

CHAPTER VIII

The Freedom of the Producer

III. FREEDOM OF ENTERPRISE

FREE CHOICE of employment and freedom of collective bargaining are the two producer freedoms of most concern to most people. But they do not exhaust the list: there remain the claims of freedom of enterprise—the freedom to go into business on your own account, to make and sell what you like for the public to buy, whether "going into business" means opening a corner newspaper shop, or floating a giant company. This freedom stands on a different level from those that we have so far discussed, for two reasons. First, it is of practical interest only to a small minority. For every hundred people who work in an employed capacity, there were, in the census of 1931, fewer than eight in business on their own account. Second, freedom of enterprise had suffered many encroachments even before the war. No one, for instance, was free to run buses in competition with London Transport, or indeed to compete with local public monopolies anywhere, or with the Post Office; and no one was free to build factories on sites scheduled as residential areas under town planning schemes.

Since these freedoms are secondary in both these senses, their relation to economic planning will be treated much more cursorily than the problems posed by free choice of employment and free wage bargaining.

In the first chapter, I suggested that there is no *inherent* incompatibility between public determination of economic priorities and freedom of private ownership of industry; and that the war has in fact been run on a combination of the two. If this experiment is to be prolonged into the peace, we are faced once again with the familiar choice between producing a given result by inducement or by compulsion—but this time with a difference. In the case of choice of employment, the issue is between compelling a person to take a particular job, or inducing him to do so; but at that point the parallel with freedom of enterprise breaks down, for there can, by definition, be no such thing as compelling a person to go into business on his own account. It follows that the alternatives with which the public authorities are faced are not so much those either of ordering, or cajoling, other people to do what those authorities have planned shall be done. The choice is between inducing other people to do something, or doing the job yourself. This means, I think, that any attempt to make the output of non-socialized industries conform to a comprehensive plan will always be a somewhat precarious affair, dependent on the maintenance of a not quite stable equilibrium. A business firm can always walk out on you by closing down. It has not, however, been proved by experience that this equilibrium *cannot* be maintained.

The range of inducements by which the production programs of business firms can be brought into line with predetermined Government plans is exceedingly varied. We have already seen, quite apart from war experience, particular industries, notably various branches of agriculture, fostered by subsidies, by restrictions on imports, by guaranteed prices, or by special remissions of taxation. It is, however, significant that most of these experiments have been directed rather towards prosperity than towards production, on the implicit theory that in any given industry there are apt to be alternatives—that the smaller the output, the greater the prosperity. In that way they make pretty dismal reading.[1] It may be a considerably more tricky business to stimulate industries which are not Government-operated into an approved pattern of expansion. Even where the expansion of a domestic industry was planned, as in the case of wheat or bacon production before the war, this was in many cases only achieved by means of a contraction of competing foreign imports. The chief exception to this generalization is residential building, which was greatly stimulated by deliberate Government subsidies; although the frequent and sudden changes of Government policy as to the amount and basis of subsidies make the word "planned" seem a little out of place in this context.[2]

War experience has certainly established that in one set of circumstances anyhow firms that are privately owned will bend themselves to conformity with a plan of great and rapid and highly particularized expansion. Critics have indeed commented, and with reason, on the resistances that have had to be continually overcome even in war; and on the centrifugal pulls which regard for their own private post-war position exercises on firms now

1. Anyone in search of really depressing reading should study the complete and scholarly account of these policies in Benham's *Great Britain under Protection*.
2. See below, pp. 132-33.

working on war production. Nevertheless, by and large, a job has been done, and the plans that have been made have in fact been carried out to Government order, though only in small measure in Government factories. When the shouting and the fighting, and the sense of urgency and emergency have died away, some of the techniques which have achieved this result in war may still be useful in adapting our existing industrial structure to the task of fulfilling the plans of peace.

In this context, far and away the greatest *inducement* used has been the assurance of a certain market, guaranteed to every firm on Government work. While the state has not, as in Russia, undertaken anything like all the actual work of production itself, it has pretty well taken over the whole business of giving orders. The peculiar conditions of war certainly make it exceptionally easy for this function to be monopolized by the state; for a very large part of war-time output is not required for the use of the general public at all, but for the peculiar and highly specialized purposes of the state's own employees in the Services. The state is, therefore, placing orders for goods which are to be used directly on its own account, not resold to the public at large; and this makes its business relatively simple. If in peace time we are to give high priority to freedom of consumption, this particular war-time pattern cannot be continued when the war is over. Government contract for goods for Government use does not, however, fill by any means the whole of the present picture. We also have extensive Government buying of goods for civilian use—notably in the food trades; and this may be a useful model for combination of peace-time planning with freedom of enterprise.

There is a large field here for experiment and exploration which is already engaging the attention of many economists.[3]

Experience also suggests that inducement can be supplemented by limited, or by negative, compulsions which may still make possible the preservation of a qualified freedom of enterprise, even where there is extensive planning of production. The fact already mentioned that a person cannot be compelled to go into business on his own account does not mean that once in business he must be completely a law to himself. It is still possible for compulsion to be applied (though of necessity only somewhat gingerly) to people who are in a position to clear out altogether if they wish. During the war, extensive use has been made of what may be respectively called negative, and secondary, compulsions. By negative compulsions I mean such methods as the control of business by systems of licensing. A power of licensing is an obvious negative method of controlling economic priorities. Thus nobody can ever be *compelled* to take out a catering license; but without such a license nobody can at present open a restaurant. Licenses can be issued freely where expansion is desired, and sparingly in cases of low priority.

More positive is the obligation now imposed on firms to manufacture or sell a certain quota of goods of a Government-specified design. In this way the production of utility goods of all kinds has been carried out through the channels of private manufacture. There is nothing in this technique which could not be transferred practically unchanged into the post-war world; and it is a direct and

3. See, again, Beveridge, *Full Employment in a Free Society*.

positive method of giving effect to deliberate plans of production.

The whole question of the relation between freedom of enterprise and planning needs to be treated as a matter more of expediency than of principle. The traditional controversies between socialists and non-socialists only obscure the practical issue which we have to face. These controversies are barren, first, because they are framed in terms not of quantitative differences, but of absolute systems. We have not seen, and we shall not see, the ideal socialist state: we have not seen, and we shall not see, unadulterated capitalism. Even the highly planned Russian economy, as has already been remarked, carries its fringe of private enterprise; and the Americans have their public utilities. Just as every economy in the world is a mixture of plan and no-plan, so is every economy in the world a mixture of the same ingredients—private enterprise, state and municipal enterprise, semi-public corporations, and producers and consumers co-operatives, compounded in varying proportions. Realistic discussion must concern itself, not with two extreme alternatives, but with the endless possible quantitative variations of the mixture.

The socialistic-capitalist controversy is barren, in the second place, because it involves a confusion of ends and means. The ultimate test of any economic or social policy or "system" is its reflection in the lives of the individuals whom it affects. The values that matter are happiness, freedom, security, and the fulfillment of individual personalities in harmony, not in conflct, with one another. It is by their ability to promote such values as these that economic "systems" must be compared: these systems are means, not ends. The assumption that happiness, freedom, security, and the harmonious fulfillment of personalities, can be realized either only where men and women are employed in the service of public authorities, or only where they are not so employed, is unsupported either by experience or by rational expectation: there is no magic virtue in public employment, no magic vice in the enterprise of the private business man; and the converse is equally true. Both public and private employment are to be judged by their fruits: and the fruits are always various. Often the way of life of individuals may have more in common with that of their opposite numbers under a different system, than with others living under the same system as themselves. The Southern farmer of capitalist America is nearer to many Soviet peasants than to the New York financier; and the Swedish farmer would both understand, and differ from, his Russian and his American counterpart. All of these enjoy, and all of them lack, certain elements of freedom, happiness and security: all enjoy and all lack certain opportunities for fulfillment of their personalities. It is by a concrete, realistic measure of these enjoyments, and not by any *a priori* theories of the inherent superiority of one system over another by which alone policy must be guided.

Even those convinced socialists who have prejudged the issue in their own minds would do well, for tactical reasons, to accept this empirical approach to their chosen goal. The smoothest path towards social ownership of industry is along the road of the demonstrated failure of private enterprise to enrich individual lives in these ultimate values. The roughest possible road, calculated to arouse the bitterest opposition and to minimize disinterested support, is a comprehensive program of socialization for its own sake. If economic planning for security and rising standards of living fails, because of the resistances and the uncooperative attitude of the business world, the case for public ownership will be strengthened beyond all measure. It is not strengthened by anticipations of such failure, unsupported by the evidence of experience.

In the end it will no doubt be the state of everybody's temper as much as anything else which will decide the issue.

CHAPTER IX

Political Freedom

THE ESSENTIAL political freedoms are the right freely
to express criticism of the Government and its
works; the right to form opposition political parties; the
right to replace one Government and legislature by another, without resort to force. All the constitutions that
are generally classified as democratic secure these rights
by one device or another. They differ in the particular
mechanics used, as also in the generosity with which they
accord these rights to all, or restrict them to a limited
class of, citizens. Ultimately, all democratic Governments
derive their mandate from some kind of popular vote,
though there is, of course, no common rule as to who may
exercise this franchise. Such matters, however, as the age
of enfranchisement, the disfranchisement of women or of
persons owning less than a certain amount of property, or
even of persons holding particular opinions, such as conscientious objectors, are, for all their importance, nevertheless secondary to the fundamental question whether
there is, or is not, freedom of political agitation, and freedom to replace one Government by another otherwise
than by force. So long as these freedoms are secured, they
can be used to widen and democratize a limited suffrage.

Without them we are all equally powerless.

The obverse of these freedoms is that the tenure of every democratic Government and legislature is necessarily insecure. The degree of insecurity varies under different constitutions. In this country it reaches a maximum, in that any Government is liable to defeat in the House at any time, is expected to resign if defeated on any issue of consequence, and has the right, on defeat, to dissolve Parliament and appeal to the country. In the absence of any such interim dissolution the maximum peace-time life of any British House of Commons is five years. Other Constitutions, like the American, provide a definite term for the legislature or executive or both, without any provision for interim renewal; or achieve continuity by providing that a proportion of the members of one House of the legislature, as in the American Senate, should retire (unless re-elected) at fixed intervals. The long and the short of it is that under the pre-war constitutions of the world the members of democratic governments and democratically elected chambers could not normally expect a life of *more than* five years, and were often liable to, and actually suffered, sudden political death, at much shorter intervals.

The dilemma that we have to resolve here is that economic planning demands continuity, and political freedom appears to imply instability. Nothing can alter the fact that we cannot both make effective long-term plans, and continually exercise the right to change our minds about anything at any time.

There can be little doubt that insistence on this right has, in the literal sense, made short work of attempts at planning in this country in the past. The most egregious example is perhaps that of housing policy in the nineteen-twenties. Immediately after the last war, everybody was agreed (as everybody will be agreed again) that a great building program was necessary, both to make good the arrears of the war years, and to clean up slum areas. Yet during the first six post-war years housing policy was made and unmade by three major Acts of Parliament, each modifying or revoking the substance of its predecessor, not to mention a series of scarcely less far-reaching administrative changes. In these conditions it is not surprising that the number of houses actually built fluctuated violently. Precise annual figures are not available before 1922: in that year a total of 91,000 was achieved in England and Wales. The next year there was a drop to just over 86,000. In 1924 the figure rushed up to over 136,000. This remarkable increase was directly due to the relatively generous subsidies made available under the Acts of 1923 and 1924—particularly the latter, which was the most ambitious of all the series. This last Act did, moreover, make a bold attempt at long-term planning. In the schedule to the Act (but only in that schedule) will be found a table of the number of houses to be built over the next fifteen years. On the strength of this apparent stability the Trade Unions even agreed to relax some of their restrictions on the number of apprentices permitted to enter the various building crafts. The scheme, however, lasted not fifteen years, but two; after which it was replaced by another plan, similar in general design, but providing a lower rate of subsidy on houses to be built thereafter. The schedule of 1924 thus remained only a paper project. The number of state-assisted houses which it had proposed for Great Britain for the year 1931 was

360,000: the number actually built (including the unassisted) was 212,000. For within two years of the passing of the 1924 Act, political freedom had thrown out one Government and substituted another of a different political complexion. To this the collapse of the fifteen-year plan was due. There could not be a better illustration of the destructive effect of unstable politics on stable planning.

It cannot, however, pass the wit of man or woman to devise means whereby some continuity could be given to those Acts of government which form an integral part of a long-term plan. In fact this has indeed sometimes been done. The modern practice of establishing by Act of Parliament permanent, or near-permanent, Boards or Commissions, with a definite job to do, is an effective way of circumventing the effects of political crises and the changeableness of Parliaments and their electors. London Transport, the Central Electricity Board, and the B.B.C. are familiar examples of such independent Boards. The details of the constitution and powers vary from one case to another, but certain principles are common to all. In particular, in every case the Board is itself created by Parliament, normally by statute, though the constitution of the B.B.C. is embodied, as befits the dignity of that corporation, in a Royal Charter. Further, the instrument which establishes each of these Boards defines both its constitution (that is, such matters as the method of appointment and term of office of the members of the Board itself, who are in effect the governing body of the whole enterprise), and the job which it has to do. There is also always provision for periodical review, on some Parliamentary occasion, of the work of every such Board. In the case of the B.B.C. a full-dress debate is devoted to this inquest, which takes place at intervals of several years on the occasion of the renewal of the charter: in other cases the matter is less dramatically staged, and is, as a rule, annually dealt with under the vote for the Government department most closely concerned with the work of the Board in question.

There can be no doubt that the establishment of these Boards has in fact resulted in real continuity. We have only to contrast the history of housing with, say, the history of the unification and development of wholesale electricity production by the Central Electricity Board, or with the eleven years' work of the London Passenger Transport Board, to see how true this is. If the business of house-building had been entrusted to such a permanent corporation, it would certainly not have been blown about as it was by the changing currents of the political atmosphere; even though it remains true, that what Parliament has done, Parliament, under our constitution, can also undo. The Act or instrument establishing any of these Boards *could* constitutionally be revoked or modified, at any time; just as every local authority in the country could, for that matter, be legislated out of existence at any time. Nevertheless it is a *fact* that although one Parliament may be ready and eager to reverse the *policies* of another (and may indeed have been elected with that very end in view), there is in practice far greater reluctance to wind up an independent going concern, which is charged with a specific task, even though this may have been established by a Government of a different political complexion. This is one of the intangibles which, in the real world of conventions, common sense and tradition, so often prove decisive.

It is clear that large programs of planned production might be carried through by extended use of such Boards. Sir John Orr, for instance, has suggested [1] the establishment of a National Food Board, charged with the duty of bringing a sufficient diet within reach of everybody's pocket. The same kind of model could be used to organize the production of any goods to which a considered plan had assigned priority.

Like every form of organization, these Boards have their own peculiar vices and virtues, which have been fully and admirably discussed elsewhere.[2] Some are better organized than others, some have better systems of staff recruitment and promotion, while in some the method and tenure of appointment of the responsible heads is more straightforward than it is in others. If the scope and number of such Boards is to be increased, these are all matters for careful consideration, in which the worst need to be leveled up at least to the standard of the best. These issues are not, however, primary for our purpose of combining political freedom with the continuity necessary for purposeful planning. From that angle (apart from the obvious retort that, by taking the services provided by these Boards out of politics, we are in fact diminishing political freedom—which is dealt with below [3]) the chief criticism may well be that this particular technique provides actually too much continuity. An independent organization inevitably develops a kind of life of its own,

1. In his *Fighting for What?*
2. See, for instance, *Public Enterprise*, ed. Robson.
3. See p. 149.

and, equally inevitably, it becomes a focus of vested interests: people connected with it want to keep it going for no better reason than the fact that it is there. It may, therefore, happen that the system of working through a number of sectional bodies, each with a specific task, will sooner or later become an obstacle to any comprehensive plan of production, in which the parts are nicely fitted together. This is certainly now true of local authorities, at least so far as many parts of their work are concerned. In the case of local authorities, however, the problem is aggravated by the fact that municipalities, which were created at one time to do one job, now find themselves loaded with a host of different tasks, which were never foreseen at the time of their birth. Nevertheless, we should take warning from the reluctance of all except the most unusually public-spirited local councils to surrender any of their powers or even to combine with others in the provision of certain services.[4] The time may come, for instance, when London Transport will appear far too parochial; and the time has perhaps already come when attempts to straighten out the method of retailing electricity will call for a fundamental reconstruction of the Central Electricity Board.

If these objections are felt to be serious, again it cannot pass the wit of man or woman to invent alternative methods of arranging the mechanics of stability under a democratic constitution. It might, for instance, be possible to discriminate between different kinds of laws, bestowing

4. According to reports in the local press in the spring of 1944, it would appear that the Borough of Henley-on-Thames, for instance, has decided to open a public library largely to forestall the possibility that Oxford County Council would open a branch of its county libraries in the town.

on some a sanctity and permanence which others do not enjoy. Already our constitution provides for discrimination between money bills and other Bills not wholly concerned with the provision of revenue, and lays upon the Speaker the duty of deciding which is which. To take another parallel, written constitutions usually require a special (and specially cumbrous) procedure for constitutional change, which has the practical effect of making such changes relatively infrequent, even though they are not subject to any specified time-table. To design, however, the exact machinery most appropriate for giving stability to laws determining economic priorities under the British constitution is a task for constitutional lawyers. The suggestions of the layman are likely to be dismissed as too naïve. But the layman certainly has a right to the opinion that this is one of the cases where, if there is a will, there is also a way.

The real question is then: is there a will? The most powerful of all criticism of long-term planning comes from those who suggest that the reason for continual changes of mind is the lack of any common agreement to give shape and direction to our plans. Since a plan without a purpose is a contradiction in terms, no group can make an effective plan unless there is some purpose upon which the members of that group are agreed, and which the plan is accordingly intended to fulfill. Professor Hayek has argued that, in modern political units, no such common agreement is possible. In his view, there is, for instance, no agreement, and no possibility of agreement, among English people as to the kind of economic pattern that they would wish to see in this country. Any conscious attempt to shape our economic life in a particular way—

to foster this industry in preference to that—simply reflects the victory of one sectional interest over another. It follows that only a tyrannical Government will attempt to sponsor any kind of economic design or plan. Indeed, planning and tyranny are, in his view, so far synonymous that the only innocent laws are those which are so general in character that their impact on particular groups or individuals cannot even be foreseen. In this context Professor Hayek draws a contrast between "laying down a Rule of the Road, as in the Highway Code, and ordering people where they are to go." [5] The effect of the Highway Code on individuals is unforseeable in the sense that the rule that all must drive on the left permits no inference as to what particular persons will be found driving in a particular place at a particular time. On this account, it is argued, the Highway Code benefits all at the expense of none. A public decision, on the other hand, as to the number of pigs to be reared not only permits, but demands, inferences as to the position of pigbreeders after the decision has been put into effect. Its whole purpose is to enrich or impoverish the pigbreeders, or to compel them to breed, or not to breed, such and such pigs: if the particular effects could not be in some degree foreseen, the regulation would not be worth making.

Since the area of genuine agreement is thus limited (the argument runs), the planner is driven to resort to improper devices for concealing disagreement, or for creating the appearance of an agreement which has no real existence. Among such devices Professor Hayek particularly mentions the practice of delegated legislation—not

5. *The Road to Serfdom*, p. 74.

only in the form in which particular tasks are entrusted
to Boards and Corporations, such as we have mentioned,
but also in the many instances in which Ministers have
power to fill in the details of legislation by Statutory Rules
and Orders. Parliamentary discussion and control would
reveal disagreement; the planner therefore by-passes Parliament by throwing the onus of unpalatable decisions on
to Ministers and officials whose actions cannot be defeated
by a critical Opposition. Moreover, as soon as Government
passes beyond formal rules "providing opportunities for
unknown people to make whatever use of them they
like"[6] to actual choice between the needs of different
people, the volume of decisions to be made becomes enormously multiplied, and Parliament gets pushed out by
sheer inability to manage the weight of its task. Finally,
in order to cover all this up, attempts are made to manufacture the appearance of agreement by dishonest propaganda, and eventually by the forcible suppression of any
dissident opinions, so that the will of a few is passed off
as the will of the majority, if not of all. Planning thus leads
to the eventual abolition of all political, as well as of a
good slice of cultural and civil freedom.

This is an extraordinarily depressing and pessimistic
doctrine. Its validity all turns on this question of the limits
of *genuine* agreement. Professor Hayek's contention that
agreement stops when we pass from formal rules with
unforeseen effects, to specific rules with foreseen and intended effect upon individuals is, of course, part and
parcel of his denial of the possibility of planning for indeterminate cultural ends.[7] It presumes an utterly skeptical

6. *The Road to Serfdom*, p. 73.
7. On which, see the argument of pp. 23-33 of this book.

attitude as to the common good. Here we have a curious illustration of extremes meeting. On the one hand is the cheerful assumption of the writers whom Professor Hayek quotes. To them the common good appears so obvious that not a word is given to its definition, or to explaining how it is to be interpreted into practical policies: to Professor Hayek, on the other hand, definition is equally superfluous since no common good exists at all.

Now, if the common good means only the literal, direct, personal, advantage of every individual, it is true that there are, in time of peace, few, if any, concrete policies or plans by which that good can truthfully be said to be promoted. This is the fact which is too glibly passed over by the uncritical advocates of "planning for the common good." In this sense, but only in this, Professor Hayek is right in his denial that, for practical purposes, any common good exists at all. Such elementary social objectives, for instance, as the prevention of unemployment or of under-nourishment are pretty sure to demand personal sacrifice from some sections of the community. Unemployment has its attractions to an employer picking and choosing in an overstocked labor market; and effective nutrition policies are likely, at least in the beginning, to involve taxation which somebody must pay. In time of war, it may perhaps be said that effective measures of defense are directly advantageous to everybody without exception (though even then, these measures cost some people a great deal more than others). There is, I suggest, no parallel in time of peace.

To show that no plan or policy is likely to redound to the personal advantage of every citizen is, however, in no way to prove either that no policies or plans can commend themselves as desirable to those who do not personally stand to gain, and may actually lose by them; or that the only "goods" in the world are those which can be literally bought and sold. It is, happily, a fact that opinions are not always entirely determined by the direct economic advantage of those who hold them; and it is also a fact that people do have definite preferences about such unsalable values as the kind of social pattern which they find desirable. Just because these values are unsalable, however, the ballot-box of the market place (as we saw in Chapter IV) must fail to count them. For by its very nature, the market is incapable of registering preferences which cannot be reflected in the consumers' demand for particular articles. One can buy a theater ticket, and so register a preference for a particular play; but, as we have seen, no one can *buy* full employment, however much he wants it. And what is true of full employment is true of all other essentially social values: that is, of all preference for one kind of social picture rather than another. The fanatical admirers of the market are, however, reduced to saying, at least by implication, that since these social values cannot be measured by so perfect an instrument as the market, they cannot be values at all.

This last assumption is ridiculous. A man may desire to live in a world where everybody (not only he himself) has enough work and enough to eat, just as keenly as he wants to see *Chu Chin Chow*, even if no objective machinery has been invented by which the relative strength of his two desires can be quantitatively measured. Different people may feel the attraction of a world where everyone has enough to eat and enough work, with different degrees of intensity, even though these degrees cannot be compared as the value of one man's purchases in a shop can be compared with the value of his neighbor's. That which cannot be mathematically measured (at any rate in the present state of the science of social measurement) does not, on that account, cease to exist, or even to matter. Social elements in the common good, such as full employment and full nutrition, are real enough. But in a complex society, where, as we have seen, every social policy is bound to tread on somebody's toes or touch somebody's pocket, they can only be defined in terms of common agreement, not of common interest; and they can only be promoted by deliberate planning, and not by any commercial market. The common good is, in fact, anything which is commonly thought to be good.

In interpreting this principle in practice, it is important not to slip into the prevalent and dangerous error of identifying the common good with the social objectives of one's own particular sect or party, and of ascribing the rejection of these by others as necessarily due to their stupid or selfish disregard of the general welfare. Opposition may as well spring from a perfectly *bona fide* difference of opinion as to the nature and content of the common good, based upon a different valuation of the welfare of certain individuals or sections of the community, as upon callous indifference to that good. It is possible, for instance, to hold that very ambitious schemes of, say, social security, house-building and family endowment would not contribute to the general welfare, if in fact they could only be carried through at the cost of a very drastic reduction in the standard of living of the relatively comfortable: the injury to those who lose may be honestly felt (and not only by the losers) to outweigh the benefit to those who gain. In practice, of course, these are always questions of degree: at some point even the most ardent reformer will pause. But so long as everybody wants to stop at a different point, so long is there real difference of opinion about the general welfare. Indeed, beyond the point of agreement, we are not really justified in speaking of the *general* welfare at all: strictly speaking there is no such thing—only a variety of opinions as to whose welfare ought to come in front of whose.

The expressions "common" or "general" welfare need, in fact, to be carefully defined. It is not enough to say that whatever contributes to the welfare of the majority must necessarily promote the common good. The tyranny of majorities is scarcely less to be feared than the tyranny of minorities. The greatest happiness of the greatest number was a good formula, and, as a definition of social objectives, it has never been improved upon, in spite of much subsequent philosophical obscurantism.[8] The real difficulty about this nice utilitarian formula is that it is two-dimensional. The greatest happiness of the greatest number can equally be the product of intense happiness to relatively few, or of milder joys to greater numbers. Counting heads is not enough. It is here that the real scope for disagreement begins. In these conditions the public-spirited politician is right to hope that the program of his party will in time command such wide approval that it comes to rank as an accepted contribution to the general welfare. But he is wrong to assert that it already does so

8. As for instance the attacks upon Utilitarian ideals in Macfie's *Economic Efficiency and Social Welfare*. If this book is not an insidious justification for cultural totalitarianism (which I cannot believe to be the author's intention) what, if it could be interpreted into plain language, would its meaning be?

rank, on the ground that everybody really wants, or at least ought to want, what he and his party want, or what he and his party think would be good for everybody. At any time the *common* good consists only of those social objectives about which there is in fact genuine and general agreement; including, it must be repeated, agreement from those who personally cannot gain and may lose in an individual, materialistic sense from the realization of those objectives.

It follows from all this that planning and effective political freedom are only compatible in so far as people are *really* of one mind about what they want to plan for: otherwise continuity could only be maintained by tying the hands of an Opposition which disapproved not only of the methods, but also of the objects, of the plan. In Chapter II it was argued that acceptance of certain economic and social aims as objectives of an economic plan is quite a different matter from submission to cultural uniformity. Indeed the achievement of such aims as full employment and full nutrition are conditions precedent to the effective pursuit by individuals of the cultural activities of their choice. So we need not be afraid of agreement. The critical question is simply: are we, or are we not, so deeply divided that there are no genuinely agreed social objectives which could be embodied in a long-term plan?

The most convincing evidence that the British people are not, and were not even in the inter-war period, so deeply divided as this, is the large measure of agreement between the professed objectives of all political parties. At the least they all now offer, with Mr. Churchill, food, work, a home to every citizen. The differences appear in what more is offered over and above this minimum, and in the parties' several opinions about methods. Traditionally (at the time of writing it is too soon to be specific about post-war election programs) the Labour Party wants much nationalizing and much education, whilst the Conservatives are more concerned with strong defenses and the remission of taxes upon business firms. But no party upholds or condones hunger, slum living, or unemployment. Either there is now general agreement that these are elements in the common evil, or somebody is telling a crashing load of lies.

Those who hold firmly to the belief that every political party is based upon a particular economic interest or class must, of course, deny that any such agreement is possible, and so dismiss, by implication, the possibility of any continuous planning without sacrifice of political freedom. As the years pass, however, it becomes harder and harder to relate each of the British political parties to a specific group of economic interests, and harder and harder to find groups sufficiently large, coherent and exclusive to make a platform for a distinct political party. We may still trace relics of the simpler pattern of an earlier age, when the Conservatives might with justification have been labeled the party of the landowners, the Liberals the party of the business men, and the Labour Party the representatives of the manual workers. The class structure of this country is, however, now so complex that if every party is to represent one class, and every class to have its own party, we shall need, not two or three parties, but dozens; and the situation is still further complicated by the fact that a realistic picture of this class structure is not a neat map in which the boundary of each class runs contiguously with the boundaries of its neighbors, but a much more elaborate affair in which these boundaries overlap, so that some territory is shared between two or more classes. All employed persons have, for instance, some interests in common with all other employed persons (*e.g.*, protection against dismissal without due cause or reasonable notice); and we can, therefore, provisionally, assign them all to a class labeled employees only. The better-paid salaried employees are, however, often so much nearer in standard of living to independent professional or business men than to their poorer manual-working colleagues, that they may well be advised to form a common front with the former, rather than with the latter, groups in defense of that standard, thus aligning themselves with an economic middle class. There may be some coherence at the top and at the bottom of the economic scale; but the middle classes are both very numerous and very heterogeneous—not so much a class as a muddle of classes. More and more, ours is a world of many little coteries, combining and recombining in complex patterns of harmony and discord; and less and less is it a world of large groups in clear and permanent conflict with one another.

Much of the present confusion of English politics probably arises from a conscious or unconscious hangover of this doctrine that each political party must be tied up with the cause of a definite economic interest, which is itself coincident with a definite group of individuals. The decay of enthusiasm for the established political parties is, in part at least, due to the fact that the traditional battle-cries no longer make sense in a world in which so many people are, so to speak, fighting on several sides at once.

Yet the malcontents with the old parties are far too miscellaneous to shape themselves into a new party with a clear class basis.

If we could shake off this hangover, we might develop political attitudes in which the limits of agreement and difference would become much clearer. At present all the emphasis is on points of difference. In political controversy it is generally customary (especially under a constitution as unstable as ours) for opposing parties to attack the *whole* of each other's program. The effect of this tradition is felt, I think, at all political levels. Discussion in the local Party meeting, just as much as in the House, tends to take the form of advocacy by the various participants of a number of views, or drafts of policy, of which one finally prevails. Right up to the moment at which a vote is taken, each protagonist is concerned *only* to win the others to acceptance of his particular opinion or presentation. Argument is concentrated on controversial debate, rather than directed to the deliberate search for the maximum consensus of opinion. The worst examples of this are found sometimes in small political societies, where the strength of each member's devotion to his own particular way of putting things is out of all proportion to the significant difference between his views and those of his fellows. It is here that the truth of H. G. Wells' dictum that no passion in the world, no love or hate, is equal to the passion to alter someone else's draft, is only too well illustrated. But, in greater or less degree, the same tendency to lay disproportionate emphasis on differences, and to ignore agreements, runs through all democratic political life. And recent history, as in the rise of Nazi Germany, has tragic enough examples to show of the

disasters that may follow when large areas of agreement
are forgotten in the intensity of conflict on the fringes.

Some modification of this attitude will, I think, be necessary if democratic governments are to undertake extensive
economic planning. As we have seen, planning is possible
without sacrifice of political freedom only if the limits
of any plan which is to be exempt from continual dis-
turbance fall within the boundaries of genuine agreement
on the purposes which the plan is to achieve. This brings
to the front the new task of determining where those limits
lie. It is not, as Professor Hayek asserts, a case of *manufacturing* agreement for the sake of action. It is a case of
discovering agreement prior to action. This is the technique in which democracy is so little practiced.

To show that this distinction between the agreed and
the controversial is not, in all circumstances, a creation
of the academic imagination, we may look at one or two
concrete examples. At the time of writing a furious political campaign is about to open in the United States.
The stormy election of the new President by popular
vote will be as unlike the meek endorsement of a dictator's
rule by conscript plebiscites, as anything that it is possible
to imagine. Yet one topic—the military conduct of the
war—on which common agreement is acknowledged, is,
by consent of all parties, wholly and explicitly removed
from the arena of controversy. Effective long-term planning will be possible when, and only when, acceptance of
certain peace-time objectives becomes as wholehearted,
and is as fearlessly acknowledged, as is the necessity of
military victory in war; even though, as we have seen,
the objectives of peace are unlikely to be based on the

same universal identity of personal interests as the objectives of war.

Here we may contrast two cases in which the policy of delegating specific tasks to non-Parliamentary Boards has already been adopted in this country with very different results. The London Passenger Transport Board was established by a predominantly Conservative Government: but the terms of the Act to which it owes its existence differ only in a few particulars from the Bill drafted by a previous Labour Government. There was in fact substantial all-party agreement that London traffic should be handled by a unified organization not responsible to, nor controlled by, private shareholders. Although members of the Labour Party may deplore as excessive the compensation paid to owners of private enterprises absorbed by the Board, and although there has been much criticism of the peculiarly cumbrous methods by which the members of the Board are themselves elected, a long-term plan for the management of London traffic has been put into effect, with general agreement, and is in essentials unchallenged. Contrast with this the attempt to take questions as to the scales of relief to be paid to the unemployed "out of politics" by the establishment of the Unemployment Assistance Board in 1934. At that time public opinion was deeply divided on the subject of the scale of allowances proper for those of the unemployed who were not eligible for insurance benefit. The subject was certainly not within the area of common agreement. This was indeed so plain that from the first the Board was given very little independence—even those who wanted to take the matter out of politics did not dare to do this in more than a half-hearted way. Thus the Board's own regulations, which fix the actual scale of allowances and methods of assessment of means, cannot become effective without express Parliamentary approval. And in fact the Parliamentary uproar created by the first set of draft regulations could not have been greater, or more politically threatening, had the proposals been those of the Minister of Labour himself, unsupported by any non-political independent Board. The Board proved a very poor shield for the Minister! In effect the management of London traffic has, and the regulation of assistance allowances has not, been successfully taken beyond the range of Parliamentary opposition, just because the one subject is, and the other is not, within the area of common agreement.

It is, of course, easy to argue that, since in fact governments of different political complexions do cheerfully reverse each other's policies when steps have not been taken (as for example with the B.B.C.) to put these beyond the range of continued Parliamentary interference, opposing parties really agree only when they are more or less compelled to do so. In this context the example of the continual changes of housing policy, quoted on p. 132, may be used as superficial evidence that no common opinion on housing policy ever existed. It will be said that if the job of house-building had been handed over to a non-Parliamentary Board this could only have meant the successful suppression of one opinion on the subject by another. Had there, in fact, been substantial agreement on the whole subject, all the chopping and changing about expressed in the successive Acts would never have happened.

This is a specious argument. Yet it does not necessarily

follow that, because successive Parliaments change their
minds and their policies, there is in fact no continuity
of opinion between them. Here we have to give weight
to that emphasis on differences rather than on agreements which, as has already been suggested, is so deeply
characteristic of our whole political makeup. Good party
capital is made not only by doing things differently from
the Opposition, but by doing as many things as much
differently as possible. And this emphasis on differences
is powerfully reinforced in Parliament by the fact that its
successful use can shorten the road to power. The way
to throw a Government out before its full course has run,
and so perhaps to get your own Party into power in its
place, is to defeat that Government in the House of
Commons. For this purpose it does not greatly matter
what the defeat is about. The subsequent general election
campaign will, as a rule, range over issues much wider
than the particular topic which led to the Government's
resignation. Opposition parties, therefore, with their eye
on early prospects of power, are naturally on the watch
to seize any and every point on which there is a chance
that they may carry a majority against the Government
in office. It is the fact of a Government's defeat, much
more than the matter upon which it has been defeated,
which in these circumstances becomes of first importance.

So long as political *tactics* demand that every disagreement should be exploited and magnified, and every
agreement minimized or kept dark, so long in fact as
the Opposition's attitude is of the old fashioned "Go-and-
see-what-the-Government's-doing-and-tell-it-not-to" type,
so long must it be impossible fairly to judge the extent of

common opinion: and so long shall we be more disposed
to under-estimate, than to exaggerate, the measure to
which we are agreed. If, however, any serious attempt
at continuous planning within, but not beyond, the limits
of the area of common agreement is to be made, some
method must be found of determining when that area
ends. We must not lay ourselves open to Professor Hayek's
charges of simulating or manufacturing agreement.

   I have said above that common agreement does not
mean majority agreement. This opens the door to slippery
mathematical arguments. If a bare majority is not enough,
how much more is necessary? Does a three-quarters or
four-fifths majority constitute "general agreement"? Or
must we reserve this expression for cases in which complete unanimity obtains, and no single objector can be
found? Here, surely, the practical test must lie, not so
much in a mere matter of numbers, as in the opinion of
organized political parties. In a political democracy, common agreement exists on those policies or objectives which
every political party will accept. Planning on the basis of
such agreement is therefore only possible, if the parties
are themselves willing jointly to define the purposes which
they have in common. This means a new kind of inter-
party conference—or inter-party-leader conference—using
the unfamiliar technique of searching for agreement, instead of magnifying differences. The purpose of such
explorations must be strictly to define, not to belittle or
to exaggerate, agreement. At any given moment agreement
and disagreement are facts. Conferences to distinguish
the controversial from the non-controversial should, therefore, be strictly fact-finding. It is just as important that
controversy should rage unchecked about matters which

are genuinely in dispute, as that it should not be artificially inflamed, for tactical reasons, where differences are microscopic or imaginary.

On Parliament then, must fall the duty of enacting the special laws, or establishing the extra-Parliamentary institutions, by which agreed long-term plans will be put into effect. If additional safeguards of agreement are wanted, it might be provided that the passage of Acts, which initiate long-term plans that cannot constitutionally be upset by a change of Government, should require more than a bare majority. Actually, however, this is probably superfluous, since if there is genuine inter-party agreement very large majorities will follow automatically. One safeguard is, however, essential. It is not the proper business of a stale Parliament to decide great issues such as the delegation of long-term planning to extra-Parliamentary authorities. The men and women who actually make these decisions must be sure that they enjoy the confidence of the men and women on whose behalf, and in whose interests, they are made. Only a freshly elected and representative Parliament can claim that confidence.

We may now sum up what all this means in terms of political freedom and political controversy. Nothing that has been suggested here touches the essential political freedom—the right at any time to remove by constitutional process and not by force the persons holding supreme political power, and to put others in their place. Nothing that has been said touches the freedom to criticize openly the actions of the Government in power, and to agitate publicly for different policies, or for a different Government. As long as these liberties are secure, there is no totalitarianism, no dictatorship. These are the political

freedoms which are lacking in all totalitarian states. Even
in the U.S.S.R. no alternative government to that of M.
Stalin can be constitutionally offered to the electors: not
at intervals of five or ten years, much less by a defeat in
the Supreme Soviet at any time. Perhaps nobody wants,
or ever has wanted, to suggest such an alternative? To that
question there can be no answer, so long as no constitutional channel exists through which an opposition could
make its voice heard. And in these conditions there can
be no answer to the charge that political agreement is
manufactured or simulated.

What I have suggested is, on the contrary, that agreement should be *discovered;* and that, where and in so far
as it obtains, so far and no further, should economic and
political programs be placed out of reach of the unstable
gusts of Parliamentary democracy. Governments will come
and go, answerable still to Parliament, and through Parliament to the electorate beyond. The only difference is that
when they go, that part of their work which has the electorate's approval will be protected from the risk of being
swept away along with that which is distasteful. This
means, I think, some quite unspectacular changes in Parliamentary procedure; and a more considerable change in
political attitudes. It means that politicians must have
the courage to admit agreement.

What the extent of common agreement in contemporary
England may turn out to be (war objectives apart) no one
can say: for, with our continual emphasis on differences,
no one has ever tried to find out. In practice some of the
most difficult issues are likely to arise where there is agreement on ends, but disagreement about the methods by
which those ends are to be reached. More people, for in-

stance, are convinced that unemployment must be prevented, than are of one mind as to the right way to prevent
it. In social affairs the line between ends and means is
not at all clearly drawn: it is indeed by no means easy
to draw. Practical politicians appear to trouble very little
about the distinction, with the result that attachment to a
particular method becomes as passionate as devotion to
the objective which that method is intended to promote.
For instance: in housing policy what matters is that good,
convenient houses should be expeditiously and economically built where they are wanted. The question whether
those houses should be built directly by municipalities or
through contractors, or in some other way, is a question
of method. The first consideration in choice of method
must always be the measure in which this or that way of
tackling a job will get the job done: and that is (after the
event, anyhow) a question of fact. The contractor-versus-
municipality issue turns, therefore, primarily on the question—in which the appeal must lie to experience—which
of the two will actually show the best performance in the
economical and expeditious building of houses where they
are wanted. There may well, of course, be no general
answer to this question, but different answers in different
social and economic environments.

It is much to be hoped that the attempt to explore the
range of inter-party agreement will lead to calmer and
clearer thinking about the distinction between social ends
and means; and to a much more experimental attitude
towards the choice of means. The desirable course is to
judge the achievements of the other parties by their fruits
(have the houses been built or haven't they? Has unemployment been abolished, or hasn't it?); and not to make

too much fuss about methods except, of course, where these may themselves violate other accepted social ends, *e.g.*, where the labor used to build the houses has been sweated, or where unemployment has been eliminated by putting people on to stupid and unprofitable work for work's sake. The danger is that in practice our attachment to particular methods will be so obstinate, and the experimental attitude so weak and rare, that the range of agreement will be unnecessarily narrowed, because those who agree about what they want to do persist in quarreling about how it should be done.

Just as no one can forecast what the scope of agreement may turn out to be, so, equally, no one can say what is likely to be the effect of continuous long-term planning within the field of that agreement, on the quality, tone and content of political controversy. The simple basic principle remains—the more people are agreed, the less there is left to quarrel about: and vice versa. It may be that eventually we too shall evolve into a one-party state. But if that happens along the road here sketched, it will be simply because agreement has encroached so far upon disagreement that the latter has become too insignificant to be worth bothering about. As long as the agreement is genuine, and the voices of dissent are in no way stifled or perverted, this would be an entirely happy ending to party strife, wholly compatible with the fullest political freedom. Such a one-party state is not the one-party system of totalitarian dictatorships. But it is also, no doubt, for a long time to come, Utopian.

In the meantime we must expect that opposition parties will have plenty on their hands. Outside the field of agreement their role will remain just what it is today—the same offer of alternative policies, programs and personalities[9] to the electorate, the same continued challenge to the Government in power. Further, even within the area of agreement, it will be the special responsibility of the Opposition to judge promise by performance, both as plans unfold, from day to day, and on the occasion of periodic searching inquests. No plan must run forever.

9. In the next chapter some reasons are given for hoping that the emphasis will be increasingly on personalities, rather than on policies and programs.

CHAPTER X

Who Is to Plan the Planners?[1]

I

IN THE preceding chapters I have tried to show that there is nothing in the conscious planning of economic priorities which is inherently incompatible with the freedoms which mean most to the contemporary Englishman or American. Civil liberties are quite unaffected. We can, if we wish, deliberately plan so as to give the fullest possible scope for the pursuit by individuals and social groups of cultural ends which are in no way state-determined. The consumer can enjoy the pleasure of comparing prices and qualities, and spending money that is freely available to the limit of his income, just as and when he thinks fit. Industrial direction and industrial conscription are unnecessary. Planning need not even be the death-warrant of all private enterprise; and it is certainly not the passport of political dictatorship. It is true (and indeed obvious) that the *same* part of the economic pattern cannot both be deliberately planned, and left to emerge as the result of the uncoordinated actions of thousands of consumers. But consumer sovereignty, in any meaningful and defensible sense, seems to be quite unattainable and cer-

1. For the wording of this title I am indebted to Karl Mannheim's *Man and Society*, p. 74.

tainly never to have been attained outside the covers of an academic textbook; and there is the less cause for tears on this account, inasmuch as no ordinary consumer would be conscious whether he enjoyed that sovereignty or not. It is true also that the preservation of free choice of employment under planning would be impossible if wages were to be settled by a private tug-of-war between employers and employed, in which each party exploited its full economic strength. But against this must be set the fact that free choice of employment will never be a reality without planning, since legal freedom of choice is a mockery if economic pressure compels the chooser to accept the first available job. The right of effective choice of employment is the one great freedom which the pre-war Englishman, or American, or Continental European outside Russia, has never enjoyed. Planning could give it to him.

A happy and fruitful marriage between freedom and planning can, in short, be arranged. That leaves us with the problem (which we have so far taken as solved) of translating "can" into "will." This is a problem of social and political psychology. Success or failure turns on the behavior of the actual men and women who have the responsibility of planning: on the measure in which positions of power are filled by men and women who care for the freedom of others and (what is not less important) in whom this love of liberty is not subsequently stifled by the habit of authority. Here, of course, there can be no secure guarantee. All the old clichés are just as true as ever they were—power still corrupts, absolute power still corrupts absolutely, and eternal vigilance is just as much the price of liberty as ever it was. The prospect for freedom is indeed bright only where these truths are fully appreciated and constantly in mind. The practical question is how best to apply these age-long lessons of experience to the modern world.

If we are to accept Professor Hayek's view that economic planning inevitably brings the worst to the top, we may as well throw up the sponge altogether. His arguments in support of this thesis are, however, happily inconclusive and unconvincing. Three main reasons are given for his fears. The first rests on the argument that "in general the higher the education and intelligence of individuals become, the more their views and tastes are differentiated and the less likely they are to agree on a particular hierarchy of values." From this proposition derives the corollary that a "high degree of uniformity and similarity of outlook" will be found only in "the regions of lower moral and intellectual standards." Any group strong enough to impose their values on all the rest will, accordingly, never consist of "those with highly differentiated and developed tastes." [2] In the second place, the number of those whose "uncomplicated and primitive instincts happen to be very similar" is unlikely to be sufficient to give a "potential dictator" all the support that he needs. It therefore becomes necessary for the dictator to convert others to the "same simple creed"; and his readiest converts will be found amongst "the docile and the gullible" who have no strong convictions of their own and whose "passions and emotions are readily aroused."

The force of both these arguments is clearly contingent on the validity of Professor Hayek's further thesis that economic planning necessarily implies cultural uniformity

2. *The Road to Serfdom*, p. 138.

and political dictatorship. They are framed all along in terms of the methods by which a *dictator* must win support in order to impose a uniform cultural pattern. If, however (as has been argued in Chapters II and IX of this book), it is perfectly possible for a free democracy to plan for cultural diversity, then these particular fears are irrelevant to the only society in which we are interested. Even that, however, is not the only answer. For it is by no means certain that what we have called the "area of common agreement" necessarily relates only to the "lower moral values." There seems to be a double confusion in Professor Hayek's statement that "the largest group of people whose values are very similar are the people with low standards." On the one hand high moral value appears to be here confused with intellectual complexity. Obviously, more people will agree to intellectually simple propositions than to those which can only be grasped by sustained mental effort; but this has nothing to do with morals. On the other hand, moral values that are "low" in the sense that they are *elementary* seem to be confused with those that are low in the sense that they are *base*. Agreement on certain *elementary* moral values, *e.g.* (apart from the special circumstances of war), on respect for human life generally and for lives of children in particular—is unquestionably widespread. Is this to be dismissed as a "low" moral standard? A public duty to protect men and women from unnecessary danger (as by factory legislation [3]), and to promote the health of mothers and children (as by a service of infant welfare clinics) is no longer disputed. Admittedly, the prevailing

3. Professor Hayek himself does not quarrel with factory legislation. *The Road to Serfdom*, p. 81.

ethic in these and other matters falls short of that set
for themselves by the most morally sensitive and unselfish
members of the community. But this is no argument
against giving practical effect to the more elementary
moral standards attained by more ordinary folk. To suggest otherwise is to imply that private virtue cannot surpass
the prevailing level of public duty. That is evident nonsense. The obligation to comply with minimal factory
legislation has never prevented public-spirited employers
from providing amenities far beyond the requirements of
any Act of Parliament. Nor have exceptional men and
women ceased to lead lives of outstanding kindliness and
generosity merely because we are all now compelled to
contribute something to the support of the sick, the unemployed, and the aged. If the many cannot reach the
standards of the few, there is no inherent law of planning
by which the *few* must be dragged to the level of the
many. In this country the standard of public morality has
been slowly rising for at least three generations, as the
higher standards of the few have become the accepted
values of the many. In Nazi Germany the worst got to the
top all right. The one experience is just as valid as the
other.

Professor Hayek's third reason for expecting the scum
to come to the top is that "it seems to be almost a law of
human nature that it is easier for people to agree on a
negative program, on the hatred of an enemy, on the envy
of those better off, than on any positive task . . . The enemy,
whether he be internal like the Jew or the Kulak, or external, seems to be an indispensable requisite in the armory
of a totalitarian leader." [4] The last sentence needs no

4. *The Road to Serfdom*, p. 139.

further commentary, since it again implies the identifica-
tion of planning and totalitarianism which this book is
concerned throughout to dispute; though even so, we
might question the logic which argues that the worst must
come to the top from the way in which they behave, after
they have got there.

The main substance of this final argument contains a
useful caution, but is not itself conclusive. Certainly it is
a common experience, not confined to totalitarian regimes,
that people exert themselves more willingly, and co-operate
better, in response to appeals to fight an enemy rather
than in simply helping one another. It may be prudent
for the constructive planner to make some concessions on
this account—to march under the banner of war on want,
for instance, rather than to sing the praises of a world of
plenty. But these are relatively minor issues. The root of
the matter is that mere demonstration that the negative
and destructive appeal is easy is no proof either that it
is the only appeal possible, or that it must in all circumstances prevail. At the most, the defeatist can prophesy
that time will show that destruction always wins. Time
has not shown this yet. But there is a challenge here that
the constructive planner would do well to meet with care
and courage.

If this is all the evidence, there seems hardly better
case for taking for granted that planning will bring the
worst to the top than for the opposite assumption that the
seats of office will be filled with angels. Our rulers are a
mixed lot. Hitler, Chiang-Kai-shek, Roosevelt, Churchill,
Stalin, Mustapha Kemal, Hansson, Alcazar, Cárdenas,
Blum, are all men who have held high political office in
recent years. No obvious correlation is apparent between

their merits (or those of their colleagues) as rulers, and
the degree of economic planning for which their Governments were responsible. In these conditions the rational
person will treat the problem as an open one, capable
of better or worse solution according as we are successful, or unsuccessful, in creating the conditions which
favor the rise to power of the wise and public-spirited
and the preservation of their wisdom and public spirit
against the corruptions of office.

In a democratic society this raises at once the question
of the proper relationship between the Government and
the people to whom that Government owes responsibility.
Western democracy has not yet settled this relationship
satisfactorily. Western democracy is, however, still very
young, and the circumstances of its infancy have been
exceptionally trying. Everybody knows that the democratic procedure works best when the questions to be
settled are within the everyday experience of those to
whom they are referred, and when those who elect understand the business entrusted to those who are elected. In
these conditions, rational judgments are likely to be
reached by a process of relevant reasoning, and the work
of elected representatives or committees will be fairly and
competently assessed. Everybody also knows that these
conditions can be fulfilled only in very small and homo-
geneous groups—much smaller than any contemporary political democracy. As numbers increase and questions
become more complicated, the part played by irrelevant,
and therefore irrational, factors in shaping democratic
decisions increases alarmingly.

Now it has so happened that the birth of Western
democracy coincided with the opening of an age of un-

exampled technical change, which no longer leaves any comfortable place for the small political unit. It is a commonplace that the whole world is now so closely interlocked that the daily welfare of any individual is at the mercy, not only of the Government of his own country, but also of economic and political events at the other side of the globe. Synthetic European rubber may ruin the Malayan planter just as Indian tariffs and cheap Japanese textiles closed the Lancashire mills. Nearly all politics are now international politics. It follows that for effective government the range of authority needs to grow wider and wider. At every level the price of efficiency is centralization. The parish council fades into near-obsolescence, while the region in its turn threatens to supersede both the borough and the county. In the United States the balance of power moves from the states to the federal government. And the independence of the sovereign state itself is already as much fiction as fact. But the price of centralization is itself a continual widening of the gap between government at the center and governed at the circumference. Hence, in a democracy, political issues increasingly outspan the knowledge and experience of the voter; and his opinion, when he has one, falls into insignificance as one unit in a total of many thousands. The simple theory that the electors instruct, and the elected carry the instructions out, becomes impossibly naïve.

The result of all this has been to impose upon the infant democracies burdens quite unsuited to their tender years. No one need be surprised if their rate of infantile mortality has, in consequence, been high. Democracy is suited to an intimate personal environment: modern technique imperatively demands government upon the grand scale. Somehow democracy must adapt itself to this inexorable twentieth-century climate. The problem is aggravated, but not created, by the fact that political responsibility has been more widely distributed than education of more than the humblest standard. An uneducated democracy is, indeed, almost a contradiction in terms. But even education is not enough. No generally attainable standard of general education can bridge the gap between the demands made upon the voter and his ability to meet them. For the issues which face (and ought to face) modern governments demand specialist knowledge: and that not only in one or two fields. The contemporary voter, if his opinions are to be taken seriously, ought to have, at the least, a considerable *expertise* in geography, history, economics, and hygiene, not to mention familiarity with the ways of life followed in any and every part of the globe. Successful education, moreover, depends upon the interest of those to be educated. The level of sustained political interest in the Western democracies has never been high: and there are signs that, in this country at any rate, it is falling rather than rising. Organizations which seek to stimulate a sense of civic responsibility by instruction in, and discussion of, public affairs have never succeeded in touching more than a tiny minority. Yet the political apathy of the majority may give less cause for despair than is often thought. For that apathy may be the expression of a sort of horse-sense. It may be the indifference not so much of those who can, but will not, as of those who realize when they cannot—a refusal, in fact, to attempt a response to demands that are recognized to be impossible.

This does not, however, alter the fact that the results

of political apathy are disastrous. Unable to give competent and informed judgments—to take only a few examples from recent history—on such matters as the wisdom of abandoning the gold standard, the pros and cons of protection, the ethics and expediency of intervention in the Spanish Civil War or of guaranteeing the frontiers of Poland, the elector ceases to attempt to exercise rational judgment at all. So we have the wives who vote as their husbands tell them to, the Scotsmen who are Liberals because their fathers were, the fanatical party adherents who are governed only by herd loyalties, and the thousands who are bullied, cajoled, coaxed, seduced or near-bribed by interested persons whose judgments are frequently no better founded than their own. In these conditions, while experience shows that the worst do not necessarily always come to the top, the choice of the best is evidently most precarious.

The problem of adapting democratic theory and practice to the realities of the modern world will not be solved in a day: it is, perhaps, the most fundamental of all the social problems of our time. One cannot hope to do more than compel attention to its importance, and offer a few hints as to where the solution may eventually be found. Unquestionably, the increased scope of governmental activity, and the increasing centralization demanded by modern technique, involve great risks, just as they also offer new and splendid possibilities. Up till now, those who are most excited by the possibilities—the constructive planners of the Left—seem to have paid astonishingly little heed to the risks. Yet these dangers, like many others, threaten most those who take them least seriously. The first step is to wake up to their existence.

The next is, perhaps, to recognize that if we cannot ourselves hope—as electors, to give competent instructions on the business of government, we must shift the emphasis to wise selection of those who can. In the preceding chapter I have tried to suggest how our present system of party politics may be adapted to the new tasks of economic planning. Any change must begin from that system, because that is where we now are. No political method is, however, immutable: and it is (in Britain even more than in the United States) the Parties which are to blame for imposing upon the elector the impossible task of judging issues outside his experience. A new relationship between government and governed which is more in keeping with the contemporary ethos, will demand more attention to the quality of our governing personnel than to the actual details of what potential governments propose. (Quality, of course, in that context implies integrity and public spirit quite as much as ability.) Most of us are already better judges of people—even of public men—than we are of public issues; and most of us could probably improve the quality of our judgment of personalities more easily than we could equip ourselves effectively to judge these issues. It follows that if in a modern democracy the elector's task is more and more a matter—in the modern slang—of choosing the right government and then letting those chosen get on with it, the political parties of the future will have to adapt their practice accordingly, giving increased attention both to the selection of their own personnel, and to education of the voter's judgment of personalities rather than of policies.

One may indeed anticipate that the system under which no qualifications whatever are constitutionally prescribed

for candidates for the highest elective offices will not last
forever. Sound democratic theory does not require that
the business of government should be as much open to
the ignorant, the incompetent, or the senile as to those
who are endowed with good faculties of which they are
still in possession. Sound democratic theory, and the protection of freedom in particular, does require that we who
are to be governed should retain the right to accept or
reject from within the field of those who have attained
a proved minimum of competence, those whose government seems to us more or less to be preferred: a right
which is the more important so long as objective tests of
integrity and public spirit lag so far behind the mechanisms (crude though these may still be) for measuring
intellectual qualities.

Further, just as we are mostly better judges of people
than of positions, so also is it easier to assess past performance than future promise. Few of us could have given
much of an opinion, in advance, about the merits of programs of food distribution and rationing, including the
control of imports and of international exchange, into
which these necessarily ramify; but the judgment of the
ordinary person that he has been well, and on the whole
equitably, fed during the past five or six years, is an
opinion deserving of respect; as its opposite would be,
equally. From the assessment of such concrete perform-
ances, rather than from boasts of coming Utopia, the new
material of political discussion must increasingly be
drawn.

In so far as the elector is still bound to judge comparatively untried men on the basis of future promise rather
than past performance (and the political newcomer can-

not, of course, be rated on his record), the chief need is for that calmer and clearer thinking about the distinction between social means and ends to which reference has already been made. The nearer we get to ends, the greater the competence of the elector. In a free democratic society, where cultural freedom, not cultural uniformity, is the purpose of planning, social ends are reflected in the final impact of plans and policies on the lives of individuals; and they resolve themselves at that point into values that are simple and intelligible as well as significant. It is the intricacies of methods and incidentals that cannot be mastered without expert and specialist knowledge. We all know the difference between peace and war, between work and unemployment, between a higher and a lower standard of living, between streets and fields, between a house and a flat: and we can give sensible opinions on such broad issues as the relative priority to be given to house or school building. But ignorance of diplomacy, history and foreign cultures makes us poor judges of particular questions of foreign relations: ignorance of economics makes us poor judges of financial policy; and ignorance of administrative and business technique poor judges of who should play what part in the execution of a building program.

Thanks to the tendency for political parties to make party capital equally out of everything—out of means as much as out of ends—little attention has yet been given to the task of presenting to the elector only those issues which are within his competence. To ask his opinion on matters where it is not, as much as on those where it is, worth having, makes too easy an excuse for treating that opinion, as in practice, equally contemptible in all spheres.

Successful political democracy under modern technical conditions will certainly demand a considerable modification of the traditional form of party programs. Simplicity and precision are the qualities most needed—simplicity through the exclusion of questions of technique and method, and precision through the formulation of definite, concrete goals (on which it is possible to hold divergent opinions) in place of promises of peace and prosperity in terms so vague that no one can dispute them. Eventually, perhaps, rival political programs may even reach a stage of precision when they are expressed *throughout* in quantitative terms. The plan of the Blue Party may offer a 20 per cent increase in old age and sickness pensions, a doubling of the opportunities for secondary education, a 15 per cent increase in house building, specified increases in death duties, and the abolition of all indirect taxation. The plan of the Green Party may concentrate on a 50 per cent speed-up in housing, postpone both educational advance and increased pensions, retain certain indirect taxes and stiffen the scales of surtax. We should then at the least be in a position to make effective comparisons both of one with another (which is impossible as long as everybody tends to promise everything) and subsequently, of promise with performance.

II

The wise selection of the men and women at the top is, however, itself only half the story. Democratic theory has, hitherto, been far too ready to assume that the politically conscious citizen must chiefly interest himself (preferably through active membership of a political party) in what happens at the top. Every local party meeting concerns itself with great issues of national policy—the public ownership of the mines, or the policy of sanctions against an aggressor state. The zealous party member forms, or borrows, opinions on these topics; and often acquires with them a certain contempt for neighbors who cultivate their gardens and their hobbies, never attend political meetings, and are innocent of all conviction, one way or the other, on national party programs.

More and more, however, must we both expect, and welcome, a shift of political activity from center to circumference. I say "welcome," because it is, in modern conditions, in the detail of planning, and in the detailed execution of plans, that the ordinary person has most of real value to contribute: and, no less, because the threat to freedom from small day-to-day tyrannies in the execution of plans that are generously designed to promote accepted social objectives is just as real as the threat from plans that are themselves devised by tyrants for the purposes of tyranny. The rude and obstructive official does not change his manners, or the prejudiced arbitrator correct his bias, merely because the scheme of rationing or wage regulation which he is employed to administer is itself just and efficient in principle and in intention.

War experience has taught us much about the fields in which the citizen may make his mark on public affairs. Great advances have been made in the technique for registering and measuring public opinion. We now realize that the casting of votes at occasional elections is neither the only, nor necessarily always the best, method of contact between government and governed. Reconstruction projects which carefully record the limits of distance of

church, pub, school, cinema, shops, or recreation grounds
respectively, which the ordinary person interprets as
within "reasonable proximity" to his home, or the Ministry of Food's collection of data on such questions as
housewives' liking for custard powder—such inquiries as
these may reflect more of the essential qualities of responsible democratic government than many a general
election. For it is increasingly through such channels as
these that genuinely competent and informed opinion
may make its way from the bottom to the top. It is true
that these techniques are only effective on the assumption that the men and women at the top are ready and
anxious to receive such authoritative guidance from the
bottom. The use of such methods is, therefore, in its turn,
half, but not the whole, of the story of the marriage of
democratic government with modern technique. But
actual experience has already begun to show how valuable
this half may be.

Some of the most important bulwarks of freedom, moreover, must always be built at the circumference of any
large-scale plan; and our conception of what constitutes
useful civic activity in a modern democracy must be revised so as to give proper place to the duty of manning
those bulwarks. The famous audacity of elected persons is
easily surpassed by the audacity of their non-elected
bureaucratic servants. Effective defense against that rude
and obstructive official, or that prejudiced arbitrator, does
not lie so much in agitation for a change of government,
as in a lively and efficient system for dealing with such
people on the spot. Every extension of government activity, and particularly every excursion of government into
economic planning, needs, in consequence, a correspond-

ing growth of small local organs to control officials, to co-
operate in the execution of centralized plans, to discover
and adjust local and personal grievances, to report on
results, and to offer suggestions for future improvement.
It will be in the service of such bodies as these, quite as
much as in attendance at political meetings, canvassing
at elections, or membership of party committees, that the
politically active citizen of the future will find opportunity to display his public spirit to the best advantage.

The possible, indeed the necessary, variety and scope
of such local organs is very wide indeed. Some are executive, some judicial, some advisory. Already we have illustrations of each from which to build: each has its own
importance as safeguard of the ordinary person's freedom.
Local Food Control Committees, for instance, enjoy
executive powers (including the right to initiate prosecutions) in the administration of the various food control
and rationing orders; and they are, by constitution, representative of the ordinary citizen. Indeed, both on the
Committees themselves, and on any sub-committees that
they may appoint, the spokesmen of the consuming public
must by law, outnumber the representatives of the food
trades. Local tribunals with *judicial* functions are generally modeled on the Courts of three Referees (Chairman,
and one representative each of insured persons and of
employers) attached to every Employment Exchange for
the settlement of disputed claims to unemployment benefit. The number of such tribunals multiplied enormously
with the growth of the state's claims upon the individual. Already such machinery is used to handle (amongst
other matters) the pleas of conscientious objectors, appeals against industrial direction or for deferment of

call-up, and claims for exemption from fire-watching. As for *advisory* bodies, their work and their number are already sufficient, if we include the national with the local, to fill a large book.[5] They range from the Import Duties Advisory Committee, which considers proposals for changes in the United Kingdom tariff, to the local committees which have the task of advising the Assistance Board about such local peculiarities as might call for modification of national scales of relief, and interviewing applicants for assistance who are in any special difficulties, or the cause of "special concern" to the Board's officers.

These examples illustrate forms of public service which should be very widely spread indeed as safeguards of freedom under planning. It is through these channels that the ordinary person can make known where the planned shoe pinches: through this machinery that he can often stop its pinching. On this account the constitution and methods of appointment of these often apparently humble bodies deserve much attention. As things are, there is some tendency for them to draw upon too narrow a circle of membership. The easiest method of recruitment is to look to the political parties for nominations; but in this way the field of selection may be unwisely narrowed; for, as we have seen, those who are politically active (according to traditional patterns) are a small, and certainly not a growing, minority of the whole public. Among them are found many persons of exceptional public spirit and unusual intellectual ability; but, they include also a number of the maladjusted who gladly take refuge from the concrete problems on their doorsteps by escape into the cloudier world of abstractions and generalities. And they certainly

5. See *Advisory Bodies,* by Vernon and Mansergh.

*ex*clude many of the public-spirited whose abilities are practical and constructive. War, and particularly air-raid, experience, has proved that sense of public responsibility, as well as qualities of leadership, imagination and organizing ability are to be found amongst many of the (in the conventional sense) politically indifferent. If the suggestion on page 166 is right, if political apathy may derive from an entirely proper sense of the limits of one's competence, then there is every reason to hope that these newer and more immediate forms of public service will make appeal to many who were quite unmoved by the attractions of political campaigning on the old-fashioned model. Certain it is that in any free democratic system of planning, the demands for such citizen service at the circumference will be very large indeed: so large that one may eventually expect nearly every citizen to serve, at some time in his life, on one or other of the executive, advisory, or judicial organs of an active democracy.

The potentialities of these democratic organs will of course depend much upon the qualities of the officials with whom the citizen bodies must co-operate. If I have said little of the problem of the selection and control of non-elective rulers, it is not through lack of appreciation of its importance, but from fear of being led too far from the main line of argument. The problems of the Civil and Local Government Services need a book to themselves: happily they are already the subject of many books written by authors with more directly relevant experience than any that I could claim. Here, however, certain principles of good government are clear enough, just as it is also clear that these principles are not yet fully operative in this country. First, the public official must not be too remote from the public whom he serves. It is difficult to be constantly vigilant for the freedom of people with whom you are collectively, as well as individually, unacquainted. The criticism that our present Civil Servants suffer from "being caught too young and tamed too thoroughly" [6] is well founded; and specially applicable to those who reach the top. Second, nearly all jobs in the world are better done if the experience and knowledge of those who have worked at them, or studied their requirements, are made available to newcomers; and if trouble is taken to select recruits with appropriate personal qualities. The methods of selection and training of our public servants are much too amateurish; and, in particular, there is still far too little imagination and vision as to the qualities and training necessary for those who have to deal directly with the public. Interviewing applicants for employment or answering the public's (often foolish) questions about rationing requires a specialized technique, just as much as drafting Acts of Parliament. And both types of job are best done against a knowledge of the wider social background, and an appreciation of the social purposes, which make them both necessary.

III

The last and greatest defense of freedom under planning lies in the quality and attitude of the people. Much has been said and written lately about the "we" and "they" relationship between government and governed, official and public. To suppose that the distinction be-

6. *A Better Civil Service* by G. D. H. Cole in *Can Planning be Democratic?*, p. 95.

tween "us" and "them" can be literally obliterated is, however, unrealistic. The official on one side of the counter is not the same flesh and blood as the client on the other, and language must and will express this difference. It is not the distinction between "us" and "them" that matters, but the nature of the relationship between the two parties. That relationship must be founded on a sense of partnership and not of fear.

We have all seen, if we have not ourselves been, the kind of person who regards any contact with authority as a contest, in which the scales are weighted in favor of officialdom. We have all seen, if we have not been, the timid who are helpless before any official form, who sign what they have not read, and for whom rights of appeal or opportunities which demand the smallest measure of personal initiative might as well not exist. And occasionally we have seen, if we have not been, citizens of a very different caliber—confident, alert and informed, yet still courteous, ready to understand and to utilize, both for themselves and for their neighbors, every opportunity which the democratic state has properly made available—citizens who understand laws or regulations which affect them and are not deterred by any occasions of official incompetence, irrelevance, indifference, or ill-manners. These, and these alone, are the stuff of which effective democracy can be made.

The spread of this attitude of what may be called democratic competence and courage is indeed of critical importance. It depends, above all, on an environment of social equality. Unhappily, in this country, with its rigid social class-system, this essential defense of freedom is still feebly held. The prevailing attitude towards authority is uncooperative, timid, and ignorant. The United States and some British Dominions have been more successful in establishing a robust level of citizenship: so, in a rather different way, have the Scandinavian and Swiss democracies. The success of the Soviet Union is more difficult to estimate, since the results of social equality are there obscured by the insecurity of civil freedoms.

The conditions of success are, however, clear enough to any who will observe the respective qualities of the helpless and the robust citizen. The one class consists, predominantly, of the ill-educated and the poor: in the other, at least a middle-class standard of education and income is the rule. A common educational background enables "us" to speak to "them" in their own language, and to understand with relative ease what goes on in "their" minds. Experience shows that this sense of equality and understanding can be realized if "we" and "they" have attained a *minimum* standard of knowledge and articulateness, without social segregation in class schools; it is not destroyed if one or other has higher ability, greater specialized knowledge or a wider culture above the minimum. The foundations of democratic confidence rest, moreover, in the quality, as well as in the quantity, of educational experience both in the home and in the school. In so far as the public authorities merely supplant in later life the image of parent or schoolmaster, we tend to transfer to the one the attitudes already induced in us in childhood towards the other. Parental domination or school regimentation is a poor preparation for championship of freedom in adult life.

The significance, in this context, of equality (or, to speak more precisely, of closely limited inequality) of income, is that, in contemporary class structure, differences of standard of living are the greatest of all social barriers. If the gulf between "our" incomes and "theirs" is too wide, we can never hope to dine and wine (or beer) together. Unconsciously, if not consciously, this will affect our mutual attitudes. Freedom will never be secure till no one recognizes others as his betters.

Social equality is, indeed, itself plainly the product of deliberate planning. The problem of freedom under planning thus resolves itself in the end into a circle that can be either vicious or virtuous: it is the citizens of a wisely planned society who are least likely themselves to fall victims to the dangers of planning; and vice versa. And all around that circle it is the responsible, the alert, the active, the informed, and the confident men and women in the street who hold the key positions.